Dying Again

thirteen years of

writing and waiting

Linda Diane Feldt

with

Barbara Feldt, Allan G. Feldt and
David A. Feldt, Laurie K. Feldt

Moon Field Press
Ann Arbor, Michigan

Published by Moon Field Press
P.O. Box 3218, Ann Arbor, Michigan 48106-3218
FAX: 313-662-5227

Cover art by Patricia Current DeSandro
Cover design by Linda Diane Feldt and David A. Feldt

Printed and bound in Dexter, Michigan, United States of America.

Library of Congress Catalog Card Number: 96-94256

ISBN 0-9652132-0-X

First Edition

Printed on recycled paper.

Dedicated in heartfelt appreciation
to those families who have given me the honor
of participating in their moments of birth and death.

Acknowledgments

This work makes it obvious where my love of writing originated — from my parents. It is a privilege to be able to showcase their work in this book. It isn't enough to bring their work to a larger audience — I also owe them my deepest thanks.

A great number of people encouraged this effort, including my friends, students, clients, and friends of my parents. Knowing that there were so many people who wanted this collection to be completed was immensely inspiring. Thank you to the readers who gave me early feedback and criticism, a loving act. These people include Jane Street, David Feldt, Allan Feldt, Laurie Feldt, Rosalyn Tulip, Shelly Chiesa, Curt Holtz, Barbara Steinwachs, Judy Meader, David Meader, Bill Zirinsky, and Ruth Schechter.

Judy and David Meader provided a special retreat for me in Arizona to do the early revisions. The unusual locations I found for writing were possible with the marvelous technology of an Apple Powerbook.

I give a special thank-you to the people in my life who observed first hand the finer differences between obsession and passion. Both were necessary to bring this book to completion.

Stephanie Ozer and Curt Holtz were close friends just before and after my Mother's death. I am grateful for their continuous support during that time.

Contents

Forward   **1**
    Threads   1

Introduction   **3**
    Mourning   5

One: The Beginning   **7**
    Heartless   9
    My First Step onto the Path   7
    First Funeral   11

Two: Growing Relationships   **13**
    Eye Glasses   15
    Sequel to a Yearbook Photograph   16
    Journey to Partnership   18
    Winding It Down   22
    The River Road   23
    6 Ways of Looking at 60 Years of Life   25

Three: Creating Ancestors   **27**
    Mother's Day   28
    Moon Watch   30
    Dear Grandma   33
    Conversations with Alex   34
    Eskilstuna, 1898   37
    Father   39
    Person Unknown   40
    Stepmother   41
    Parting Ritual   43
    Fathers   44
    Dissonance   45
    A Furnace Memory   46
    Bad Mother   47
    Show and Tell   49

Four: Care of the Dying   **51**

The Psychologist Writes to the Cardiologist   52

The Cardiologist Responds   53

Portraits   54

Object Lesson   56

Dying Again   57

The Unweaving   61

Thank You Letter   62

Should We Hold a Meeting   63

Letter to Allan   64

Power Transfer   65

Options   67

Regeneration   68

Expulsion   69

Five: Dreams of Life   **71**

Introduction   71

Dreams of Life   72

Serenity   75

River Dreams   77

Control   78

Packing Up   79

Six: Waiting and Wanting to Die   **85**

Live and Let Live   86

To Counter Pain   88

Indian Summer   89

Perspective   90

Without You   91

Memories   91

The Generic Letter   92

Suicide   93

Therapy   94

To the Unfinished Work for Regent Sarah Power   95

A Conversation with Maxine Kumin   96

Family Suicide   98

Essay   99

Untitled   100

Seven: Finding Peace   **101**

     To My Dear Family and Friends   102
     Dear Molly   103
     Sharing Writing   104
     Pulse   107
     Inspiration   108
     Out of the Valley of the Shadow   109
     Should I Wear a Wreath   111
     Priorities   112
     Sharing Yourself   114
     Entangled   115
     Just Keep Laughing   116
     Hailstorm   117
     Meditation on the Master Plan   119
     Dreaming of Paradise   120

Eight: The End   **121**

     In the End – Shock   121
     Journal Entry   125
     Memorial Service I   127
     Memorial Service II   129
     Memorial Service III   132
     Memorial Service IV   133
     Journaling   134
     Giving Away   136
     Thirty-Nine   138

Afterward   **139**

Index of Titles and Authors   **142**

Approximate Chronology   **143**

Forward

Linda Diane   ◆   *April, 1993*

Threads

I am standing in the back bedroom of my house untangling thread. There are spools and spools of thread, which until recently belonged to my mother, who died less than three weeks ago, just a few days past her 60th birthday. Now, because she is dead, they are mine. Some of the spools I pick up feel familiar, and I can imagine they are the same spools I bit pieces of thread off of when I was first learning to sew. Even years later, she would scold me by saying "use your scissors!" whenever she saw me bite thread instead of cutting it.

I remember those first projects she supervised of doll clothes and sock puppets. Some of this thread is on old wooden spools and the stamped prices are so low I know that I am right, I have used this thread before.

Why didn't she keep the spools more neatly wrapped? I wonder, and I am suddenly angry. If she had put each spool away properly I wouldn't be the one left doing it now that she's gone. No one would have guessed that her drawer of thread was such an unnecessary mess. As I mingle our collections together, I proudly note that my thread is all contained and the ends are caught up in the slits in each spool put there for that purpose. To keep the sewing drawers neat.

The trash container is topped by unraveled thread I've discarded. I look in the drawer and I can no longer tell which spools are mine and which are hers. It is only an hour later when someone calls to talk about last weekend's lovely memorial service that I realize the metaphor that I have engaged in this morning, and the tears come to my eyes. I've been experiencing the surprise of emotion welling up when I least expected it, and not when I planned for it, like when I spoke at her memorial service.

I like the tasks of moving her things around, giving things away, sharing with my brother and sister, finding where to put her jewelry and clothes in my house, seeing her empty closets and finding the house she shared with my father begin to be different. He puts the dishes there, a vase now stands where she would never have left it. They are the tangible ways that show she is gone.

Having her stuff merge with my stuff is my way of integrating her death, taking into my life the sudden change of not having a living mother. I've always been told that when someone dies you feel a hole, a loss. She hasn't been gone long enough to be missing, there isn't a gap yet. There is a new something in my life, though. It is a shape that I can't exactly see, and whose boundaries I have yet to know. It is a shadow being, which both removes light and life as well as reflects what I thought I knew with strange distortions and contortions. Every morning, since she died, the first thing I do when I wake up is check, and this new feeling is still there. It's becoming more familiar, but every day it is different as well. Throughout the day I feel this presence, and explore a few of its many facets.

There is no loss yet, rather it feels that I've taken on more. The pain, the grief, the confusion, there are new big feelings in my life. Where can I put all these feelings? Where do they belong as I buy groceries, talk to the U.P.S. driver, go to a dinner party, visit a friend with her new baby?

I have a new drawer of thread. More than I will use in my lifetime. All of the thread my mother accumulated in her life. And I know I'll never touch that spool of repulsive green. Or neon orange. But there is a spool of pale lavender that inspires me to take on a new project.

Introduction

On April 5, 1993 my mother, Barbara, died just a few days after celebrating her sixtieth birthday.

She had been planning and expecting to die for just over thirteen years since her first heart attack in March of 1980. She was left with congestive heart failure and a gradually diminishing life-style. She became a writer at the end of her life.

Her reasons for writing were many. She wanted the attention certainly, the fame and recognition. She also sincerely wanted to help other people who were also going through what she was experiencing. She found that writing about her ongoing depression, her occasional thoughts of suicide, her past difficulties with raising her children, her disability and struggle to cope with a terminal illness — all of these subjects had audiences she found were eager to hear another person's intimate perspective. She hoped that she could help others by writing about what she was experiencing. When she heard from other people that they had been touched by her work she was overjoyed. It meant everything to her.

I love my mother's poetry. Much of it is still very evocative for me and I continue to learn about her and her feelings by reading it again and again. Her words speak clearly to me. I have found traces of sly humor or quiet rage that speak to the difficulties she had in coping with being terminally ill. Her writing has insight and wisdom as well as the passion of someone who knew that she would soon be leaving her words behind for later and unknown readers.

I'm not sure that she ever let herself truly hear the praise that I and others had for her work. She wanted her poems to be liked and appreciated. Her strong need for adulation may have interfered with being able to accept the praise when it did come.

During those thirteen years and after, my father Allan also began to write again. An academic at heart, he took up the art to explore his feelings as well. A lot was changing in his life as he began to physically care more and more for his terminally ill spouse.

My father's poems came more sparsely than my mother's. He didn't feel the self imposed pressure of having to write everything before it was too late. Each of his poems was loaded with emotion and expressed feelings that we weren't used to hearing him express, in any form. The first time I read one of his love poems to Mom I was shocked. I realized with that one poem that I had misjudged and misunderstood an important part of who he was and how he felt. It is a pleasure to give his work a larger audience as well.

We were a family of five. I am the middle child with an older brother, David, and younger sister, Laurie. We each wrote as well, especially following traumatic events in this long death process.

This is a story told by the poetry my mother and father wrote in the last decade of their life together. It is also told in the short journal entries, stories, and letters she wrote, and in the short stories and words that I have to contribute as well. My mother had begun a book, she called "Dreams of Life." I have included excerpts from that work.

My brother and sister have contributed a few "afterthoughts" that help to represent a small part of their personal perspectives. Although we shared the experience of my mother's death together, it was very different for each of us. This book is an assemblage that is my viewpoint, and not necessarily theirs.

My mother wanted her work to have a larger audience. What we experienced as a family as we went through the dying process with her is not unusual or even particularly special. Sharing the story from five perspectives through poetry and short stories is unique and I believe very special. This isn't a chronological account. It's a story made up of stories. It is our story about living and dying.

Allan ♦ *April 7, 1993*

Mourning

Two days after they wheeled your
lifeless body away for cremation
I am strangely at peace.
Can mourning end so soon?

Then I recall climbing an Arizona trail
to visit old Indian ruins twelve years ago.
Overcome with grief, I realized that never again
could you join me in such a climb.

My heart wept nine years ago when
you arrived so exhausted by a five hour
flight that we needed a wheelchair
to move you through the busy airport.

I shared your sorrow four years ago when
you resigned the part-time job you loved.
Even in a wheelchair you could no longer
endure a half day's work at the office.

Two years ago we gave up plays and movies
as too exhausting to be enjoyed any longer.
That year we also gave up Christmas trees
and tokens of love stronger than a hug and kiss.

Now you have given up the last faint traces
of your life, Barbara. But you were forced
to yield so much in earlier years that
this final loss pales in comparison.

Together, we have mourned your losses
for over a decade while your life
slowly ebbed away.
Now it is done. Mourning is over.

The Beginning

Dad called me around 11:00 PM on March 10, 1980. I remember just a few things about that call. I know he told me that Mom had sustained a heart attack and he was calling from the emergency room. He told me it was serious, and in a very straightforward informative voice — almost neutral but with a background of fear and shock — he said she was O.K. for now but the future was unsure. I remember the sensations. The bottom of my stomach first dropping and then tightening. My arms moving in front of my chest, fists clenched, in some protective gesture. And I remember that I wasn't alone — that I told my then boyfriend that my mother might die. I felt shock as I said the words in answer to his question, "how is she?"

I was standing in the back room of my apartment, in a room with a cement floored shower you had to step up on, a washer and dryer next to that, and a laundry sink that was my only kitchen and bathroom sink. Remembering what a weird place I was living in will always be associated with my mom's heart attack. It's all lumped together now in time and space. Remembering that room (in my mind's eye) is feeling for the first time that Mom might actually die. That she almost did.

This is the story that began that night. Of how she lived and prepared to die for the next thirteen years, and how we — my father, my brother, and my sister, also lived and prepared for death.

Barbara ♦ *April, 1990*

Heartless

A badly damaged heart
stabs me in the sternum without warning
thumps and bumps instead of ticking smoothly
takes away my breath when it's most needed
slows my steps upon a slope so slight
only a rolling marble could detect it.

After it has harassed me all day long
demanded dozens of green and purple pills
fed me brown rice instead of steak
how does my heart dare
intrude into my dreams?

> *My friend and I are playing bridge*
> *with my husband and his partner.*
> *I have a very good hand*
> *three aces and two kings*
> *but my husband bids three no trump.*
> *Even though he has lots of hearts*
> *And I have none*
> *I take five tricks and win the game.*

If life is like a game of bridge
how will I choose to play my cards
with a transplant my only possibility
and the donor bank as heartless
as the hand that I've been dealt?

Barbara ◆ *1992*

My First Step Onto the Path

If death is the moment when dying ends, I have been waiting for that moment for more than twelve years; sometimes impatiently, at other times praying to postpone it until a special event has been completed, but always aware that it is imminent. Dying has been a constant and major part of my life work since I suffered a serious heart attack three weeks before my birthday in 1980. I was 46 years old.

That evening I attended a monthly membership meeting of the family counseling agency where I worked part time, led a discussion of the pros and cons of a proposed staffing change and drove a colleague to his home. As I packed for a long weekend in Washington, DC, I began to feel very ill. First came vomiting and diarrhea, then sweating and weakness. I described the symptoms to my husband, and we awaited further developments. When I experienced pain in my left arm, he called the doctor's answering service. I was shocked to hear him say "I think my wife is having a heart attack." This had not occurred to me as I had never heard of a woman having a heart attack.

When the doctor called she said, "Take her to the emergency room or call an ambulance." I was frightened enough to choose the ambulance, but the possibility of death didn't occur to me. It did occur to my husband riding in the front seat, watching me lose consciousness several times. During the sixteen days I was hospitalized through many complications and emergencies, the possibility of my death was still not on my mind.

However, as cards, phone calls, and flowers arrived from family and friends all over the country, I thought a lot about my father's death. He went to work one morning, was taken to the hospital with apparent indigestion and died of a heart attack within three hours. I knew nothing of this until several hours after I returned from school when my mother came home to tell me he had died. He had no symptoms or warning prior to his death at age forty two. I was sixteen, a high school senior and my brother was a nineteen year old college sophomore.

I remembered the days we spent at the funeral home, visited by hundreds of people who loved and respected him, many we didn't even know. I wished he had been able to receive the advanced medical care which was sustaining my life, so that he, too, might know how much he was loved. I was so overwhelmed by the outpouring of love I received that I feared I might become a permanent invalid to enjoy it longer. Illness provides a rare, legitimate reason for adults to be taken care of, and I loved being taken care of. When I had gall bladder surgery eight months after the heart attack, I was so afraid the perquisites of illness would impede my recovery that I told everyone there must be no cards or gifts. It worked; I recovered more quickly than expected.

There is no privacy in hospitals and during my days on the heart floor I overheard several discharge conferences. The patient's wife was required to be present (all patients on the floor but me were male) as the doctor and nurses explained how she was to feed and care for him at home, and what rehabilitation and job retraining resources were available to him. When I left there was no request for my husband's presence and no discharge conference. No one asked what kind of work I did. I was given written instructions and sent home to take care of myself. This was my first experience of gender discrimination in the field of cardiology, a problem finally acknowledged by researchers and practitioners within the past few years.

I left the hospital feeling that my heart was a ticking time bomb, primed for a fatal explosion. I knew it would happen, the only question was when. I had no idea how to live with this feeling. I needed to talk to others who had experienced heart attacks, particularly women, so I tried to find a support group. While the Cancer Society has all kinds of groups for patients and their families, the local hospitals and the Heart Association offered nothing but pamphlets. I was urged to start a group myself, but did not have the physical or emotional strength to do so.

I continued seeking support and assistance and finally found a Polarity Therapist and a Clinical Psychologist who provided what I needed. But for many years I did not understand the special and unique qualities of the journey I was embarking upon, a search for a way to live in enlightenment in the shadow of death.

At the age of fifty two, after seven months of therapy, I was able to visit my father's grave for the first time. I had insisted for thirty six years that there was no reason to do so, because he was not there. I was truly amazed at my reaction on finding my grandparent's headstones next to his. Of course I knew that they had died, but I had not attended their funerals and I never thought about their burials. Yet I was overcome with happiness to see them all there, together. I experienced them as living people, reunited and existing cozily side by side. Somehow this vision changed my attitude toward their deaths and my own. The walk through that cemetery became literally my first steps on a path of conscious living. Six years later when I discovered the healing qualities of writing, I was able to transform the haunting memories and fears surrounding my father's death, which had kept me from accepting my own mortality, into a poem which dispelled their power over me.

Barbara ◆ *1991*

First Funeral

I am in a child-sized Sunday School chair
hearing you read the week's lesson,
giggling about "suffer the little children".
    Not here on a hard wooden funeral chair
    listening to Reverend Beck abridge your life.

I am in bed listening to Heidi's adventures
lumpy mumps forgotten in your soft hug.
    Not here in the women's rest room,
    an aunt's bony arm around my shoulders
    as I disgorge my grief into the toilet.

I am at Cowden Lake, admiring a string of perch,
laughing at your toes corrugated by leaky waders.
    Not here, mesmerized
    by an unnaturally wrinkled thumb
    embalming has failed to plump.

I am on my knees in the garden
ready to grab the fishing worms
turned up by your spading fork.
    Not here beside your grave, dreading
    the first shovel of dirt on your casket.

I am reading a bronze plaque thirty six years later,
for the first time, because I believed my father was
    not here in this barren graveyard.
    Yet I am filled with joy to discover
    his parents are here with him.

Growing Relationships

My parents were high school sweethearts Their somewhat conventional marriage with three children was profoundly altered by illness and disability. My father was the breadwinner, my mother a full time mother and "housekeeper". Her role was to cook and clean and raise children, doing some volunteer work on the side. My father was the successful professor whose work involved late nights, business trips, and socializing within the university community.

My brother was the first to shake things up by having trouble in school and later involvement with drugs. I chose other coping tactics and somehow escaped from much of the painful acting out that he was so talented at. I was driven to excel, to identify myself by my success, and chose a career in which I experienced intimacy with clients — while distancing myself from close relationships with friends and loved ones.

My younger sister did not fare as well. She went through a recovery of her own, and through it all she related to our parents very differently from David and myself. As the youngest child, she stayed more emotionally connected to them even as her behavior was more flamboyant and distancing. All three of us posed a huge challenge to my parents, and we pushed them hard to learn and to grow. Until my mother's illness, nothing challenged them as much as ensuring the survival of their children.

Their lives did not unfold as they expected.

After we all left our parent's home as adults, we worked to establish a different type of relationship with each other. My mother and I had a professional relationship when we both held staff positions at a local runaway crisis center. My father and brother shared enthusiasm in simulation gaming and consulted on a number of projects. Laurie was still living at home when my mother had her heart attack and so had a different experience of that time than David or I. Even after moving out she remained especially close to my parents and they were involved in her life *and helped her out in many ways. We all continued to live in Ann Arbor and David, Laurie and I had time over the years to try out different friendships and ways of relating to each other.*

My parents continued to grow and change, a process that was hastened by Mom's heart attack. At age 46, my mother had not imagined that she would begin slowing down her life and eliminating options. The only foreshadowing of this was her own father's death at 42, from a sudden heart attack.

With Mom's up and down physical abilities, the patterns and routines of my parent's lives were altered. My mother the caretaker had to allow herself to be cared for. She had to learn to accept the way my father chose to do the laundry. He renewed his once dormant cooking skills. And of course, the nature of their intimacy was changed by illness and age as well.

Barbara   •   *January 14, 1993*

Eye Glasses

I acquired bifocals
the day I became
a grandmother.

They create a wall
shutting me off
from intimacy.

I remove them
to kiss my husband
the way I once took off
my clothes.

This poem was one of the assignments from a poetry class Mom took with Dad. It is written in a classical style, called a villanelle. In this style there are two rhymes and usually five tercets and a quatrain in which the first and third lines of the opening tercet recur alternately at the end of the other tercets and together as the last two lines of the quatrain. My mother loved learning about the many forms of poetry as well as using the medium for her expression. I imagine that creating a poem in such a proscribed form was a challenge similar to her love of crossword puzzles.

Barbara ♦ *May, 1992*

Sequel to a Yearbook Photograph

Sitting together thinking they are smart
Voted by peers, acknowledged in the book
Believing that they will never part.

Sharing love words shyly, of the heart
Hidden from teachers in a secret nook
Sitting together thinking they are smart.

Struck in unison by Cupid's dart
Too young to recognize the hook
Believing that they will never part.

Nothing will upset their apple cart
Future promised in a soulful look
Sitting together thinking they are smart.

Proceeding in a wedding march
Bound by solemn vows they took
Swearing that they will never part.

Joined until this life they shall depart
Not regretting others they forsook
Sitting together knowing they were smart
Trusting that they will never part.

Barbara and Allan
Tonawanda High School, New York, 1949

Journey to Partnership

My wedding was in the Evangelical United Brethren Church of Grand Island, New York on January 30, 1954, but my marriage began with a phone call one afternoon in May 1955. The wedding was between semesters of our senior year of college. We were so young that while enjoying a sunny, snowy walk the state police, receiving a report of runaway teenagers, tried to pick us up. Only our university IDs saved us from spending the rest of our honeymoon in youth detention. So we returned to our classes, libraries, and term papers; college students playing house.

Shortly after graduation, my mother became ill and I couldn't refuse her request for help. Home again in my old room I felt more like a daughter than a wife. And soon after I returned to Ann Arbor, the Army snatched Al away to basic training, leaving me alone and still wondering what marriage was all about.

Finally, after six months of training, Al moved to his permanent assignment at Fort Benning, Georgia. He found a place for us and was ready for me to join him. I quit my job, moved out of my apartment and camped out with a friend while awaiting the call that would tell me our long separation was almost over. We had agreed to meet halfway between Georgia and Michigan, but a week end pass was an uncertain commodity even when the Korean War appeared over. It depended on a concurrence of three things — all his work done perfectly, the Colonel not needing his radio operator, and the higher ups making no unexpected demands. When this happened, he would call and I would move out.

In the meantime, my mom arrived from New York to drive to Allegan, Michigan to visit her father in the county old folks home. The county home was ancient and smelled like slightly mildewed old books, but my grandfather was content. He recognized us and seemed glad to have us there, even for a short time. We returned to Ann Arbor the next day, just in time for Al's call. Although I was not ready for another drive, I packed all my household goods and parted from my mother once more. I headed south in a car so loaded I was surprised it could move.

Disaster struck first in Monroe — a blow out in the first twenty miles. I was lucky to be almost across the street from a gas station (no interstate highways then, to rush you past small towns) so I drove plunk, plunk, plunk across the street. The tires on my old car were so bad that I had two spares, both buried under a load of pots, pans and dishes. A little money and a lot of kindness put one of them on the car and me back on the road as it began to get dark. I was happy to have a gun on the seat beside me — not the real gun Al had insisted I carry and I knew I would never use, but a squirt gun filled with ammonia. This was a gun I would dare to use if needed to protect our meager belongings.

Although a lumpy mattress couldn't deprive me of my allotted five hours of sleep I was still not ready for what Ohio had in store for me. Were they repairing all their roads at once? Even the detours were under construction. During my weeks of planning for this trip I had researched the route numbers, mileages, and major landmarks with great care but soon found my lists useless. This was uncharted territory, and nothing in my previous life had prepared me for it. I crawled in a direction I hoped was Kentucky, a dusty snail with the rendezvous time coming closer and closer.

When I finally left torn up Ohio for the blue grass of Kentucky I discovered a new impediment — hills. Again I lacked experience; I had never driven on narrow winding roads that curved and climbed at random. Any bird flying over would have recognized the novice at the head of a long line of cars following impatiently behind. It felt like half the state's population was honking angrily as they passed at every opportunity. When I finally reached Lexington another kind gas station attendant directed me to the bus station. I was trembling with exhaustion and relief when I disembarked at last in the adjacent parking lot. I was afraid to leave everything I owned at the mercy of anyone with a rock, but even more worried about being late.

Although Al's bus should have arrived before me, he was not in the waiting room. My first reaction was panic. Was Lexington the destination we had agreed upon so many weeks ago, or was it Louisville? Had we ever really planned this major step in our life or had we just assumed we knew where we were going? I tried to distract myself by reading recipes in Good Housekeeping magazine, but I jumped at every arrival announcement. After two hours, I was convinced I was in the wrong city. What could I do to find my husband? Could I drive all the way to Columbus alone, and if I could, how would I find him there? I didn't even know our new address.

I tried to be calm and rational, to make a mature plan even though I felt like a lost child. First I would call the Louisville Grey Hound terminal and have Al paged. If that didn't work maybe the local office of Travelers Aid or the U.S.O. could help a lost Army wife find her missing husband. Perhaps there was an Army base near by where someone could help me make contact with Al's unit at Fort Benning. All this planning consumed an anxious hour, just long enough for the next bus to arrive from Atlanta. Fearing another disappointment I tried to stay in my seat, away from the window where I could see the bus unload. But without consciously moving, I was there, and he was there at last.

Hugs alternated with explanations, kisses combined with tearful tales of real and imagined disasters as we compared notes on how we had finally come together. There wasn't much time left on that precious pass so we dashed to the car and started out on the last stretch of our journey. "Al," I sighed, snuggling as tightly as I could, "If you hadn't been on that bus I would have begun an official search for you."

"Good thing you didn't do that," he laughed. "Our marriage would have been postponed one more time while I did time in the stockade. When I finally got on a bus in Atlanta I read the rules on the back of my pass. On a forty-eight hour pass you can travel only 50 miles from your base."

I have always had mixed feelings about my parents and the parenting they gave us children. Learning about their backgrounds, the parenting (or lack thereof) that they received, and their extreme youthfulness when they married and began their family, helped me to have more compassion for their confusion and failures.

There were areas of parenting they excelled in — teaching values, ethics, and a sense of community and the importance of giving service. They both modeled being responsible with money, doing work you love that is meaningful, and the joy of learning. These things too must have been a part of their upbringing.

I learned that one of the greatest gifts a parent can give a child is to model continued growth and learning. My parents went through a dramatic evolution in their relationship as they coped with the challenges their children brought home, and yet the most significant challenge was the spectre of death that was with our family for thirteen years.

Allan ◆ *1988*

Winding it Down

We came into this world, you and I,
As Hoover was giving it up to Roosevelt.
Early years of scrimping and saving, then years of
air raid drills, savings stamps, scrap drives.

Hard to believe we're the veterans now,
boring, yet intriguing younger friends
with our *You are There* view of history.
Murrow and Cronkite, good-night David — good-night Chet.

Now we're beginning to drop out of the race,
winded but satisfied with our run.
As we stroll placidly, watching clouds and moon,
others fly past us, intent on prizes no longer important.

We've done it all and enjoyed it greatly, you and I.
Kids, grandchildren, and old friends stop by and say hello
with satisfying ease and pleasure, showing
mutual respect uncluttered by duty and form.

Forty years together doesn't seem much
but it's three quarters of our lives, paced out
in daily doses filled with shared moments.
Sorrow and joy, triumph and defeat, passion and boredom.

If we started over, I think we'd do it the same way again.
But would we bother restarting, having done it once?
There's fulfillment and satisfaction at this end of life
that others can't understand or believe.

Thinking back on your freshness and youth,
who would have believed that you'd go first?
Warm thighs and firm breasts you pressed against me
at junior proms, graduation balls, and under marriage sheets.

The game is nearly over, a few more hands to be played.
Then we'll put away the cards, and toss out the score pad.
We've played well together, you and I
and I'll remember you always as I play on in solitaire.

The theme of transition, change, and "winding down" was prominent in my father's early poems. Writing about change was a wonderful way to stop and reflect, and became a part of the process of letting go and saying good-bye.

Allan ♦ *April 3, 1990*

The River Road

Everyone has a road somewhere that has special meaning:
the street they grew up on, a high school drag strip,
the lovers' lane where they explored youthful passions,
a road traveled daily to work, the track to a favorite fishing hole.

Special to me is the River Road just outside of town
which I first came to know as a college freshman.
One sunny football afternoon, I skipped the game
for a peaceful walk out city streets to the river.

Strolling beside quiet waters I crossed a narrow bridge
and headed back towards town along the River Road.
As afternoon heat built, I rested in the cool shade
of an apple tree, reading and then falling asleep.

Waking to a late afternoon chill, I followed the River Road
back to campus where fellow students celebrated
victory against some school whose name I have long forgotten,
though I still remember the apple tree.

Later trips out River Road led to illegal beer parties
college songs and friends surrounding a campfire,
canoeing in shallow waters, watching birds and sunsets,
taking pictures of dates — one of whom became my wife.

After graduation we rented a cheap apartment out of town
and drove daily along the River Road back to campus
where we held onto low paying jobs while adjusting to
married life, growing debts, and independence.

After fifteen years of army, grad school and first job,
we returned to the River Road, teaching at our alma mater.
Our old apartment was gone in a jumble of steel and concrete.
The two lane bridge was now a four lane expressway.

We drove out along the River Road frequently after that
canoeing with our children, feeding ducks,
taking sick children to the new hospital,
visiting wealthy friends living above the river.

Nine years later I sat beside my wife as an ambulance
careened along the River Road to the hospital.
Following her heart attack I drove that route
for weeks to visit and comfort her — and myself.

Over the following years we journeyed out the River Road
to that hospital far too often. Angina, palpitations, surgery,
sometimes staying for hours, other times for days.
Turning onto that route began to fill me with dread.

But other trips out the River Road still were happy.
Sunday afternoon drives to familiar scenes, visiting
newborn grandchildren, attending courses in music
and writing which added new meaning to our lives.

In remaining years we'll continue to drive out that road
which has been central to our lives for almost forty years.
The River Road has taken us to important destinations,
some of endings and death, others of beginnings and fulfillment.

After her first heart attack my mother literally lived to write. She cared more about her poetry and prose than anything else. Her obsession was painful for us who had other agendas for how she might live her last few days or weeks or years with us, but nothing could sway her from her mission to write to her death, which she did. The computer screen left on, with the time of the last "save file" recorded, told us that one of her last acts before she died was finishing a poem about turning sixty the week before.

Barbara ♦ *April 5, 1993*

Six Ways of Looking at Sixty Years of Life

If you are sixty years old today
What should you do about it?

You could look at pictures, decade by decade.
A wide-eyed infant, a sassy ten year old with braids
A twenty year old U. of M. graduate and bashful bride
A thirty year old mother of one boy, two girls
A forty year old harassed by teenaged dissidents
A fifty year old enduring heart deterioration.

You could take credit for a thriving, growing family.
A husband sharing a thirty nine year marriage
Three adult children living within three miles
Three happy, active grandchildren who visit often
A former son-in-law, a soon to be ex-daughter-in-law
who still consider you a friend and relative.

You could review accomplishments of jobs done well.
Meticulous coding of boring surveys at Survey Research Center
Families salvaged through painful counseling sessions
at Ozone House runaway and family services agency
Research findings instigating changes in policy for appointing
and retaining women and minority faculty at the U. of M.

You could reread documentation of efforts to improve the world.
Evaluation reports demonstrating success at Community High,
Middle Years Alternative which kept the programs alive
Ozone annual reports of services provided to desperate clients
A chapter in *Women in Higher Education* introducing a new measure of
equity. Three chap books of intimate, loving poems.

You could relive the achievement of personal growth.
Painful hours of family therapy with recalcitrant teenagers
Difficult, continuous work in personal therapy
Reading twenty self help books and following instructions
Workshops on conscious living and dying, successful couple
relationships, problems of women in their middle age.

You could relax, relate, and enjoy your party.
Eat catered sandwiches, patés, dips, and carrot cake
Graciously receive gifts of flowers, wine, poetry books
Watch Michigan win the semifinal basketball game
while "The Victors" is played on a miniature mouth organ
Exchange joyous hugs with friends and family, celebrate being alive.

Creating Ancestors

My parents were committed to conscious dying. They utilized the opportunity of my mother's illness to explore their relationship with each other, to delve into feelings they probably would have otherwise left uncovered, and to sometimes shock and educate others about death. They spoke about it openly. They planned how they wanted to die. They agreed to assist each other if necessary. They pre-bought a cremation contract and openly and honestly instructed each of us children on what to do when — not if.

The dying process also gave them an opportunity and the incentive to explore their past, their feelings for their parents, and to evaluate the totality of their lives and their childrearing experience.

Perhaps the following "Mother's Day" poem deserves some explanation at the onset. A few family friends have found it to be negative, spiteful, and wondered at how I and my siblings felt in reading it. I feel fine. My brother and sister and I were not easy children — our family did indeed go through hell, and the fact that we all survived and grew up relatively intact is impressive.

While the acting out (involvement in drugs, suicidal gestures, and other trauma) was the domain of my siblings and not myself, I can respect my mother's need to, in some way, say "to hell with all of you." Part of her healing is expressing her disappointment in this short fantasy, and having the opportunity to more publicly mourn what had happened within our family. She was bitter and angry with what she was forced to endure, and she also benefited in countless ways from the whole of the experience.

Barbara ♦ *August, 1990*

Mother's Day

I

Her belly swelling, growing
responding without volition
giving, always giving
her life's substance.
Her breasts, too, swell
flowing with milk
on demand.
Love and pride rise
with the yeast of the child
Her mind and heart expand.

So much to learn.

recognizing a rubella rash
treating scraped knees and bloody noses
why the sky is blue,
the floor colder than the rug
rituals for burying dead turtles
words to ease the pain
when invitations fail to appear
new math, computer spread sheets
nuances of funky fashion
pantomime communication
when ears are Walkman plugged
turning apron strings into elastic bands.

A mother's mind and heart
may be more crowded than a pregnant belly.
Still the possibility of growth
quickened by her children
and their children
is not lost.

II

She had survived one more
disappointing Mother's Day
too much food, unwanted gifts
her children drinking and smoking
speech like knives
stabbing and cutting each other.
But it was the day after Mother's Day
which was circled on her calendar.
The day she secretly anticipated all winter long
when it was safe to assume
all danger of frost was past
and she could move her infants
out of their protected nursery.
Since first implanting the tiny seeds
in the fertile growing medium
she had nurtured them
lovingly controlling their environment.
Wearing her prettiest flowered dress
she carried the flat of tomato seedlings
to the garden. Her trowel,
bent and scratched, scooped out holes.
She gave each plant a drink
of nourishing transplant solution
dressed it in a pleated white bonnet
for protection from the sun.
Last year's crop had failed
to produce the bounteous harvest
she expected as a fitting reward
for months of devotion
but her special, private Mother's Day
had come again
bringing another chance for offspring
who might develop
in a way that would make her proud
to be their mother.

My parents knew that soon they would eventually be ancestors, dead many years, remembered (hopefully) by grandchildren, children, other relatives and friends. Neither of them had ever said much about their own antecedents other than a few brief synopses of their lives, but both my mother and my father began to write of their grandparents in ways that betrayed their supposed lack of care or memory.

Barbara ✦ *January 19, 1993*

Moon Watch

Silver dollar size, crafted
of gold, my grandmother's watch,
my treasured possession
for thirty six years,
hers for fifty or more.

The cover is etched with leaves,
flowers, and the initials
of her maiden name, *AEW*,
Alice E. Wright. I never knew
her middle name; Alice is mine.

Broken when I inherited it
the watch cannot be repaired.
I imagine a ladylike
ticking much gentler
than a man's ponderous beat.

When I was a child
I did not touch
the round gold watch
pinned on grandmother's
left breast, over her heart.

It was as unreachable for me
as the heavens for my two year old
son who ran down the driveway,
arms outstretched, trying
to clasp the full moon

nested safely beyond his grasp
high in the dark velvet sky.
Now the watch occupies
its custom fitted niche
in a dark blue velvet case

and the moon, etched with faint
pictures like the cover
of grandmother's watch, pulls me
with the force that creates tides,
toward a role I cannot fill.

She was the ideal grandmother.
Sons, daughters-in-law
grandchildren, gathered from nearby
cities and distant states,
celebrated all holidays at her table.

overweighed with her own noodles
bread, green sweet pickles
red and purple preserves
roasted meats and poultry
rich gravies and sauces.

She sewed by hand lace trimmed
dresses and bonnets for my dolls,
cherished and entertained me
with cookies, cakes and tea,
adages and homilies to live by.

A flawed replica of my grandmother
I am no longer able to provide
holiday banquets or tea parties.
I will leave to my granddaughter
not a watch but a memory,

the irregular ticking
of a loving heart
damaged beyond repair
an eclipsed moon, at times
too dim to illuminate her path.

After working on each poem, my mother would proudly distribute copies of her new work for our praise and delighted response. She was particularly pleased with <u>The Moon Watch</u>, and told me it was one of her best. When I first read it I hated it. In comparison to her earlier work I found it contrived, sappy, and too obvious.

Knowing this would not please her, I delayed any response for a number of weeks. She finally noticed my lack of comment and pressed for my response. In sharing my feelings she let me know that I was wrong, and that it was good poetry. She was clearly offended by my observations. I had failed to remember that she wanted praise more than criticism.

Although the impulse was always present to placate "my poor dying mother," I resisted it most of the time. We couldn't go on if I was supposed to be nice all the time, and I wasn't willing to give up the benefits of being real with each other. But sometimes it would have been easier to let it go. I knew that she could die at any time and had frequent reminders of her vulnerability in the form of hospital stays and frequent stretches of bed rest. It was a constant challenge to decide which issues and feelings to let go of and which to pursue with her even if they might cause more upset.

This time, she got the last laugh after her death. In the process of dividing her possessions, I was ruled ineligible to receive the watch because I hadn't liked the poem that described it.

Mom was partly kept alive by her grandchildren, my brother's three children. She loved being a grandmother, and had the fondest childhood memories of spending time with her grandmother. As time went by, she had less and less energy to spend with her grandchildren but would occasionally spend time one-on-one with them.

My mother created a special version of this next poem for her mother, whom every-one called Bunny, in which all the references to "Grandmother" were changed to "Mother." Bunny was very touched and pleased, which was only one point of the deception. My mother was frustrated by Bunny's lack of interest or comment on her poetry, so this was also a successful tactic to guarantee a positive response.

Barbara ◆ *July 8, 1992*

Dear Grandma,

I had a tea party today
with my granddaughter, Alex.
She is six. We used the child-sized
china you gave me. Remember-
beige with pale blue rims
branches covered with blue flowers
gracefully arched like Ikebana.

A teapot, sugar, creamer,
the cake-plate's rim pierced
in two places for handles,
six plates, saucers, cups thinner
than eggshells; only one cup
is broken.

We baked cream puff shells,
filled some with tuna salad,
some with peppermint ice cream.
The cinnamon apple tea smelled
like your Dutch apple pie.

I pretended to be you
so I knew just what to do
to let a little girl know
that she is loved.

Love and kisses
from Barbara

Conversations with Alex

I have one granddaughter, Alexandra, who is four years old. Her brothers, Ian, who is eight, and Ingraham, almost one, prefer to keep moving—crawling, trotting, running; but Alex likes to sit beside me on the sofa to chat. She confused me completely one day a few months ago when she asked, "Gramma, where is Graham's shower thing?"

"Alex, I don't think I know what you mean. What are you talking about?"

"You know, Gramma. His shower thing. He's getting big now and he likes to take a shower with Daddy. He needs it. He got it for his birthday. At the party."

"But Alex, he hasn't had a birthday. He isn't one year old yet. Maybe you had some kind of party at your other grandma's. Was there a party and I wasn't there, and that's why I don't know about this shower thing?"

"No. You were there. Don't you remember? Lots of people were there. At our house. It was a birthday party."

"Well, I think I would remember if I was at a party for Graham at your house. Maybe you mean the shower when he was a baby? When great grandma was here from Seattle. Is that the party you're talking about?"

"Yeah, the shower thing party."

"Oh, Alex. There was no shower thing. That's just what you call a party for a new baby when you shower him with lots of presents. Graham got some cute clothes at that party."

"Is that all? Just clothes? Gramma, can we do a puzzle?"

A few weeks later Grandpa and I took Alex with us to the community farm to pick up our week's share of vegetables. She was in a happy mood, alone in the back seat singing, "Chicken lips and lizard hips and alligator eyes, stir them all together, it's grandma's soup surprise" and other silly nursery school songs. When we drove through Dexter she saw a tall structure near the feed store and asked what it was. It was hard to explain, but I tried.

"It's a grain elevator to store corn and wheat to feed cows and pigs."

Then we passed the cider mill, and she asked what that was.

"It's a cider mill where they squash the apples to make them into cider."

"Gramma, how do they get the apples up there so they can squash them?"

"Well, I don't know exactly, but maybe the farmers carry them up in big bushel baskets."

But Alex had it figured out. "They could use the elevator!"

"No, Alex. Remember? I said the elevator is for grain, not people."

And of course she answered, "Apples aren't people."

Then she started singing her own song — "Apples can use the elevator. Apples aren't people. They can go up and down, and up and down. Sticks can use the elevator. Sticks aren't people. They can go up and down, and up and down. Stones can use the elevator. Stones aren't people. They can go up and down, and up and down."

Poor Grandpa, laughing so hard he could hardly drive. I was glad to have a seat belt to keep me from falling off my seat. But that's how it goes when you have a conversation with Alex.

Eskilstuna, Sweden, 1898

Eskilstuna, 1898

Almost a century ago, my grandfather posed
six of his eleven surviving children
outside the farmhouse near Stockholm
in which he was born sixty years earlier.

His two youngest sons, including my father,
sprawl on the grass before him. Missing are
the two wives he buried in the Lutheran
churchyard and his five oldest sons.

Their world seemed stable and predictable.
Victoria ruled in England, Bismarck in Germany,
Sweden controlled Norway, and the battleship Maine
floated peacefully in Havana's blue harbor.

Who could have imagined the transformations
that would occur within the next few years?
Victoria and Bismarck dead, Spain defeated, Norway freed,
farm lost to gambling debts, family transported to America.

As my age matches his and I face the turmoil
of my own end-of-century, perhaps he sends
a message across the generations, "May your
new century be less interesting than mine."

My mother and father began to date seriously just before my mother's father died. She later understood how much she had used Dad to transition from being her father's favorite to Dad's. My father's mother died of complications from diabetes when he was 12, and his father just a few years later. His father had lived on just long enough to bring a stepmother into the house. My father's childhood ended prematurely and abruptly.

Allan ◆ *May 7, 1991*

Father

Like other poets, I too must probe
that aching tooth that was my father.

Youthful indifference and early death
shroud what he may have been.
I'll never know who he was
or what he would think of me.

Hand-me-down stories
trace the skeleton of boy and man.
Motherless at birth in Sweden,
boyhood spent on the family farm.

Ellis Island at twelve, migrant laborer at sixteen.
Marriage and children in his twenties.
Factory work and poverty at thirty.
An extra child born at forty.

Depression's worst blows eluded
in reasonable comfort and security.
Respectable Presbyterian Elder, source
of jobs and handouts for needy neighbors.

Widowed and aging in his fifties with
palsied hands and dribbling chin.
Easy target for a callous teen
who scorned his pain and loneliness.

Never attaining sixty, he left little behind
but vague memories and a new overcoat.
I look with envy at my adult children who
have become friends with their father.

Allan ◆ *May 27, 1992*

Person Unknown

Seeking memories of my mother,
unspent grief overwhelms me.

A moment's passion in her forties
returned her to childbirth's bed.

Damaged by my birth, she cared as best she could for me
and older children, kept alive by doctors and insulin.

Clinging to life 'til war's end reunited family,
she then welcomed death's release.

As neighbors left condolences and casseroles, a twelve year old
watched for chest to rise, eyelids to flutter.

Older than her at her death, now I realize
I never knew her as a person.

What clothes did she wear?
What books did she read?

Did she dance and sing?
Tell jokes and laugh?

Was she pretty?

Did she love me?

Stepmother

Preying mantis swathed in black,
rouge and powder masking sallow jowls,
on spindly legs she stalked into our home.

It took but a year to cajole the empty hulk
of her fourth mate into a new will and
another seven months to put it to use.

Childless in earlier marriages, she was unable
to mother the sullen teen she also inherited.
He soon fled, taking with him only sour memories.

At a garage sale held with her fifth husband
my older sister in disguise managed to buy back
a few books and dishes from our earlier home.

My mother never felt close to her own mother. My father had adopted Mom's mother as a substitute parent by default. My grandmother was a difficult woman for both of them to be close to, let alone be affectionate with. In contrast, Mom described her relationship with her father in glowing terms. She had been his favorite, his sweetheart. It was from him that she felt affection and approval. His abrupt death, just as she was beginning to explore her sexuality, was a confusing and terrible time for her.

There was certainly much sorting out and feeling to do. Many decades later, the medium of poetry gave both of my parents a wonderful outlet for beginning that process.

Barbara   ◆   *1990*

Parting Ritual

Glance in the mirror
to fold ankle socks just right
check polished saddle shoes
apply a modest trace
of Creamy Coral
run for the school bus.
She is arrested by her father's scrutiny,
his affectionate protest,
    You have too much lipstick on.

Some mornings they play
a variation on the game.
She presents herself
for inspection without lipstick,
a tube of Tempting Tangerine
hidden in her purse
to be applied on the bus,
but still he says,
    You have too much lipstick on.

Friday she dresses carefully
for a date at the drive-in movie
though no one will see
polished pennies in her loafers,
a fuzzy blue sweater
accenting her pleated plaid skirt.
The evening is launched with,
Have a good time and
    You have too much lipstick on.

If he witnessed her return
four hours later,
realized that her clothing
masked hickeys like indelible lip prints,
smudges of Passionate Peach
transferred
from her lips to her breasts,
he would surely cry,
    You have too much lipstick on.

Fathers

Although father/daughter relationships have been presented in hundreds of fiction and non fiction works, I am still amazed at how much influence my father's life and death have over my life. It is said that women frequently try to marry their father, and I tried especially hard. In fact, the night my father died my mother told my steady boyfriend, whom I eventually married, that he must take care of me from now on. My husband is very much like my father in important characteristics such as warmth, humor and absolute integrity. He is, however, a fallible human being and cannot possibly achieve the standard of perfection I have set for him.

It is not surprising that I turned to my $70 per hour rent-a-father, my therapist, as the next substitute. He listens to me with total attention, understands and empathizes with my every feeling and problem, and leads and advises me gently and knowledgeably while making no demands based on his personal needs or feelings. There is no doubt of his unconditional love. What more could one want from a father?

There are undoubtedly many more things involved in a real father/daughter relationship, and I wish I could experience them. When I see my husband interacting with our children, I am extremely envious. They are so fortunate to have a real father, despite his imperfections. He is always available to them — to listen, to discuss problems ranging from plumbing to business ethics, to move appliances or entire households, or just to brighten their lives with a new joke.

Barbara ◆ *March 21, 1991*

Dissonance

I had a doting father.
With his kind and gentle way
he couldn't even raise his voice
to make the kids obey,
    Sings little sister.

I had a wrathful father
cruel as a city cop
who beat his standards into me
with a leather razor strop,
    Sings big brother.

That was not my father.
My father was a saint.
I know I would remember
such want of restraint,
    Sings little sister.

You were not the perfect princess
nor I a complete disgrace.
You must remember how it was
and forgive your own mistakes,
    Sings big brother.

We had a loving father
the damage that he wrought
came from human weakness
the snare where he was caught,
    They sing in concert.

Legacies come in many forms. With some, we will never be able to ascertain their origin or reason. It is up to the next generation to say no. This is not my burden to share or to pass on.

Barbara • **June 28, 1992**

A Furnace Memory

In the cellar's deep recesses
at midnight while the family slept
I discharged my monthly obligation,
a ritual purification by fire.

Cracked wide the smoldering furnace,
cast in the obscene objects,
damped the harsh clamor
of the closing door

to avoid arousal of the males
who lurked to witness my discomfort;
to evade my brother's smirk,
his crude, "you're on the rag again."

What indignity was thrust upon
that nascent woman, my mother,
that she found these natural
discards too unclean to mingle

with chicken bones, coffee grounds
floor sweepings? What drove her
to forge a regulation that
bloodied napkins must be burnt?

Can I have spread this stain,
this legacy of shame,
to a third generation,
the daughters of my blood?

Barbara ♦ *October 13, 1991*

Bad Mother

Preparing to move from the house
where we raised our children
I saw on the framework of the archway
between my dining room and kitchen
a series of marks,
labeled with names and dates,
recording the physical growth of my children.
I taped together a long piece of tissue paper
traced the markings on the wall
to take away with me.

I live two thousand miles from my mother
despite opportunities to move
to her side of the country.
I don't want her near enough
to observe me raising my children
to let her hang out her balance scales
to weigh the evidence.
On one side that flimsy piece of tissue paper
to balance the heavy pile on the other side -
notes of complaint from teachers and principals,
hospital records of suicide attempts
and a nose broken by a boyfriend,
newspaper clippings of a rape,
juvenile court summonses,
bills for hours of therapy.

My mother might add her recollection
of a granddaughter who ran away
when she came to visit us
even though she never learned
that she ran to escape the pressure
I placed on her to act normal
for the two weeks of that visit.
Her ultimate judgment might be
that I should have worked those twenty years
and let some day care expert
raise her grandchildren.

My mother did not write much else about her mother. I believe that it was partly because she had chosen not to explore that relationship further. She did not want to forgive, or to open herself to her. They were a poignant pair, which I was often caught between. "Don't tell your grandmother..." "don't tell your mother...." Each was preparing to die in separate parts of the country. Travel was no longer possible because of illness and their own individual heart disease which was also a shared legacy. They seemed to be in some bizarre stubborn competition as to who would die last, each claiming that her death would be too hard for the other to bear. I had the fantasy that they might die within hours of each other, never knowing who had "won" this strange battle of wills.

I urged my mother to reconcile with her mother before it was too late. It was the one relationship that she deliberately chose not to heal. When she died, my mother had not been able to say to her own mother "I love you."

Barbara ❖ *March 16, 1993*

Show and Tell

I used to think saying "I love you"
was easy and didn't mean much
but showing love was hard
and expressed a lot.

When I was young no one said
the words but I knew my father
loved me and was sure
my mother did not.

In high school I told Al I loved him,
easy when carried away in a passionate
embrace. He didn't say the words
but I didn't notice the lack.

Now he often says, "I love you"
and I say, "I love you too."
I feel guilty I didn't say it first
but my actions tell him how I feel.

I notice that for the past year
when my mother leaves a message
on my answering machine
she ends with "I love you."

I am surprised to hear
those words from her.
We never say them
directly to each other.

Maybe if I bought her an answering
machine I could say "I love you" at the end
of the message. But she's always at home
the phone within reach of her bed.

Perhaps one of the most painful phone conversations I ever had to endure was talking to my grandmother the night my mother died. Being a responsible daughter, I called Mom's brother right away to let him know what had happened, and to ask him to tell Grandma. I waited a few hours and then called her.

I can still hear the sound of her voice in my memory. The pain and loss was incredible. Neither of us was prepared for the intensity of her emotions. All of the preparation and bucking up for this possibility fell away. This was a woman who had lost her only daughter, and her sorrow belied the estrangement that they both had shared but refused to acknowledge. My grandmother never seemed to fully recover from that night. We spoke of my mother on only one other occasion.

Grandma never asked how I was, or the rest of the family. She never acknowledged that it was my loss as well. She died in December 1994, a little more than 1 1/2 years after her daughter. She won the contest.

The only other conversation I had with Grandma concerning Mom was within a few weeks after my mother's death. She mentioned a dream that she had just before Mom died. In her dream, my mother came and visited her from "the beyond." In the dream my mother had died and came to tell my grandmother how wonderful it was and to encourage her to join her.

According to my mother, her mother had never shared a dream with her before. But they had a chance to talk about this dream in one of their last phone calls. Mom had responded that if her mother died first, then she hoped Grandma would do the same for her — come tell her how wonderful it is. They laughed about it, but in just a few weeks the first part of the dream came true. My mother was dead. Grandma claimed that she now felt less afraid to die, knowing that her daughter was on the other side to help her. But she clung to life still and to the end gave every indication that she was very afraid to die.

Care of the Dying

The strain of the day-to-day care of someone who is terminally ill is almost incomprehensible to anyone who has not been through it. My mother was more healthy than ill, but that status could change in a moment and frequently did. There were seemingly endless trips to the hospital, decisions about medication, attempts at therapies when success was difficult to evaluate, years of hard decisions and monitoring of conditions.

There were times when my mother debated, shall I go to the hospital or just stay home and die and have it over with? Such a debate betrays the ambivalence of having to undergo therapies that both sustained life and that she found ultimately dehumanizing. Her pain was intermittent. There were times when she seemed to be confused and couldn't remember things well, but although these were alarming signs they did not progress noticeably. She was frequently frustrated with lack of mobility, but even this symptom would suddenly relent and she would be able to walk short distances for a week or a month.

It wasn't such a bad way to die compared to what many others have had to endure, but it was not easy. For any of us. She was still dying, and we all knew it.

The following pair of poems are based upon actual letters.

Barbara • *March, 1991*

The Psychologist Writes to the Cardiologist

Dear Doctor,

Our mutual patient
is well known to me
more or less continuously
over the last several years.
Our objective has been
to increase her adaptive response
to her cardiac condition;
"attitude adjustment"
regarding the disability,
the rehabilitative possibility.

She has learned to dance
by the light of death,
has become a poet
in her creative coping
with life threatening illness.

There are short periods
when she is sad,
does not participate fully
in life. At times she
is close to being seduced
by secondary gains of illness;
being cared for, relieved
of internal and external
performance demands.

I do not see her
as a chronically
nor a clinically
depressed person.
She is coping well.

The Cardiologist Responds

Dear Doctor,

From my superficial analysis
you describe her status
very accurately.
The psychogenic factors are real
but not unexpected.
The problem is that she
is not incapacitated to the degree
where she would be
an acceptable candidate
for cardiac transplantation.

There is nothing more
that can be done
using conventional
medical therapy.
This is the problem.

Your attempts to help her
adapt to the situation,
at least for the time being,
are helpful.

The following paired poems are about my mother and her therapist. He was a very significant person to her for many years, and was one of the relationships she was most reluctant to end. They shared a level of intimacy that she doubted she could sustain with others. Even within the therapeutic relationship, the concept of dying changes the goals and objectives that she might have set for herself under more "normal" circumstances. They both knew that their therapeutic relationship would end by her dying, not by conventional termination.

Barbara ♦ *October, 1992*

Portraits

I am an opal
an iridescent jewel
confetti colored
softly glowing
lighted from within.

I am a pot of stones
polished by much buffeting.
An ample container,
unadorned, enfolds
my independent parts.

I am an Oriental poppy,
a brilliant orange flower
which brightened the lives
of those who experienced
my full blooming.

As my petals dropped,
they formed a pleasing
pattern. Now just a pod
subdued in color, poised
among green leaves

I am pregnant with words.

You are a daffodil
rising when the world
is bleak and cheerless,
a gleam of sunshine.

You are an English cottage,
a welcoming garden,
inside, a fire
and a cup of tea.

You are a hot fudge sundae
with mint ice cream,
warm and comforting
with a sparkling aftertaste.

You are a cat,
cool and confident,
loving and accepting love
on your own terms.

You are a channel marker buoy.
When my canoe overturned
in turbulent waters
I held fast to you.

Barbara   ♦   *January 19, 1993*

Object Lesson

I think I'll hire Christian Dior to design my hospital gowns
and ask the lady in admissions to do my colors
    along with my insurance forms.

The gowns will be the proper size and shape
    to show that I'm a person.
They will come in different colors, all chosen
    to flatter my skin tones.
They will have elaborate Velcro closings,
    no missing ties or lumpy knots to lie on.
Like T shirts, they will offer a choice of slogans
    to express my feelings.

Read my chart! I already answered those questions.

Do not awaken to administer sleeping pills.
I ♥ my phlebotomist.

We are doing very well, thank you.

Linda Diane ◆ *September 15, 1992*

Dying Again

It was the phone call I both hoped for and dreaded. We've lived on the edge for so long. Do I want it to be over or would that pain be worse? I just don't know anymore. But my father's voice was grave, his words factual. My mother was hospitalized, rushed there by ambulance, possibly she had suffered another heart attack, the doctors don't know yet. Tests were being run, it is very serious, come and see her, we'll know more later.

I stopped by for a brief visit, feeling the much too familiar anxiety and stress upon parking and entering the hospital lobby filled with patients in various stages of dress, noticeably worried family members, and sometimes a newborn baby being taken for a first car ride home. Every time I walk in that automatic door I say to myself, "I'm spending much too much time here lately." I had spent the night there just the week before, providing support and comfort to some friends through a particularly difficult birth.

Once I reached her room a monitor showed a strong heartbeat and an oxygen tube made breathing easier. We chatted briefly, I listened carefully as she told me the story of how her day had gone. There was the high drama of the speeding ambulance ride to the hospital emergency room counterbalanced with the waiting and waiting and giving repetitions of her long and difficult medical history of the last ten years.

A few hours after I arrived home my father called again. This was worse. Mom's heart had stopped as a doctor was taking her history and they had to revive her. "We almost lost her" were the words he used. She was moved to CCU, the Coronary Care Unit. We moved in with her.

There is a policy about only visiting for 15 minutes, and we never asked permission to violate that policy, we just did. And no one said a word about it. Someone from our family was with her from then on — taking five or six hour shifts. We had so many close calls over the last few years, we were primed and ready to do those last heroic acts, to be with her as she died a good death, to go the final mile. I had alerted my friends, who had all assured me that if I needed anything I had only to call. It all seemed so dream like, yet starkly real — waiting with her, watching monitors, helping her in the bathroom, watching nurses struggle with inserting and changing her IV, laughing at the hospital's version of food.

The night I stayed over with her she was cut off from food and water in preparation for a diagnostic test the next morning. I was almost sleeping on the fold out chair next to her bed, and around 3:00 AM it was obvious that she was in pain. She was also thirsty, scared and very miserable. I whispered that I thought I should sing her a lullaby. She said she thought that would be lovely.

For the next few hours we took turns singing softly together and to each other. All the old Pete Seeger songs from my childhood, folk songs that we both knew, and a lovely version of "Swing Low Sweet Chariot" with soft harmony. I sang her favorite song "The Water is Wide" which she requested we sing at her memorial service. It was a very intimate and special few hours. I was at peace, knowing that when she died in the next few days we would have shared that time together. Added to all the other talks and resolutions we had found over the last few years, it made for an almost perfect ending.

Except that she got better.

She came home. We had another Christmas. And she saw her bulbs bloom that spring as she turned 59. She lived to see one of Michigan's coldest summers. She is seeing the fall colors one more time.

It's been almost a year. A good year, an important year for her to be here and to be part of the family. So much that has happened couldn't have happened without her, my sister being able to buy her first house, caretaking for her grandchildren as my brother's marriage went on the rocks, the two of us clearing the air on old issues during hospice counseling, giving me advice on remodeling my kitchen. But I know there will be another phone call. Another wash of relief and dread. More times that are so beyond simple intimacy that the world as I know it stops, right in the midst of being with that other person. There will be at least one more storybook ending, at least one more marshaling of my friends and support people to help me through so that I can be strong and clear with my family.

This is a very strange way to live. And it's not the kind of dying that you read about in the Sunday paper magazines. It isn't very uplifting anymore. It's exhausting to be as conscious and as wonderful as possible all the time. To want to resolve every issue, to finish all the fights. To videotape her life story, and ask all the questions that I'll want to ask when it's too late to ask. Living with impending death is incredibly confusing.

I go for days not considering it, and then notice how it creeps back into my life, sometimes obviously — like being so angry with my mom and calling her a jerk, sometimes by just not washing my dishes for a week. This last spring I lost track of responsibilities and promises I had made, I had to finally admit I couldn't handle the complexities of my life. I let go of a lot of my volunteer work and extra projects. Over the summer, with no recent crises, I picked many of them back up again. This fall I'm tentatively enjoying being busy and doing more, wondering in the back of my mind how long it will last. Bracing myself for what comes next.

This hospitalization was very different for my mother as well. This time she had died, to be revived again. She had a near-death experience. A significant shift occurred after that experience. She was calmer and more sure about death. Like many who have had a near-death experience, she felt a greater peace about what might be ahead for her. At the same time she felt that she had experienced something that also separated her from others. It's hard to say if she was truly removed from those of us who have not had this coming back to life experience, or if she used that distancing as a part of the process of getting ready to leave.

Barbara ◆ *September 13, 1992*

The Unweaving

The essence of my being
appeared as a basket
woven of thin willow strips.

My heart stopped
my lungs filled and I gasped
for air. With each breath
I saw a strip spring free.

All were released
the empty base revealed
I recognized the end.

"I'm dying," I said
but my heart disagreed
and resumed its work.
Did I return to refill

my basket? Gather
daffodils, dirty dishes
dust bunnies, dreams

hummingbirds, garden
weeds, painted
Easter eggs, Christmas
cookies. To fulfill

my assignment? Capture
memories in stories,
poems, warehouse love

a lifetime's supply
for each of you
until you say
enough, and set me free.

Barbara ♦ *September, 1992*

Thank You Letter

Dear Dr.,

I think you may remember the patient you were with on Saturday evening, November 30, 1991. You were doing a history when I had a complete heart failure. I want to thank you again for your prompt and effective intervention. After my week in the hospital it was two months before I felt as well as I had prior to the heart failure. But a month ago I had a sudden and enormous improvement in my condition. I haven't felt this well in at least two years. I have been driving, grocery shopping without a wheelchair, baking cookies with my grandchildren, and even planning a trip with my husband. I have no idea why this has happened, or how long it will last, but I am certainly enjoying myself while I can.

I wanted you to know how well I am doing and also to send you the enclosed poems. For several years I have been writing poetry to help me deal with the ups and downs of my life and it has been very helpful. The experience of dying or being near death was very visual, just as I have described it in "The Unweaving". It was important and meaningful for me, but difficult to share with other people who haven't experienced it. I have also found it hard to be with people and not mention what happened to me. So the poems are a way for me to clarify my feelings and communicate them.

I am eternally grateful that you were with me and were able to bring me back for whatever time I will have to complete my life. I am enjoying every minute.

Barbara ♦ *February, 1992*

Should We Hold a Meeting

Last week when we first met
you asked, why the wheel chair?
I told you about my heart
when it stopped, started again
how alien I feel being the only one in the room
who has died.

Yesterday I learned
you were raped, beaten
left for dead.
You didn't tell me.
Don't you ache to find
others who share the link
that binds us

like a bandage?
I might put an ad
in the paper,
start a group.
Would you come?
Would anyone?
We all have places

in our lives
where something ended
and started again.
Should we get together,
or is there nothing
of consequence
to talk about?

This letter arrived after her death from the woman who she wrote about in "Should We Hold a Meeting." It was exactly the type of feedback she would have wanted to hear.

July 1, 1993

Letter to Allan

Dear Allan,

I'm not a poet (which probably has to do with not letting myself work at it) but I am an appreciator of poetry on all sorts of levels of myself. As I read Barbara's "Should We Hold a Meeting", I cried, realizing afterwards that my tears came from the comfort of her recognition of what we had in common, and more powerfully from the sense of loss; that we'd not come to know one another better. I want to tell you, Allan, that I'd had such a drawing to know her and had sought for "excuses" in my mind to go by and visit her a year ago when we were up north. Sometimes reticence and fear of bothering get in the way of knowing and loving. So I've suffered the loss of someone I would have valued as a friend. I do believe in bonds that we form with God that transcend our time and space, so I count on Barbara accompanying me there— especially as she chose to support us here.

The final line of "Dreaming of Paradise" is perfect; it caught my breath. Your "Without You" so aptly poses a question that I've often struggled with: the desire to share and almost the fear of the other's lack of *disponabilidad*. Solitude and community . . .

With loving affection,

N.

When my mother first began to cope with her illness in 1980, the concept of a living will was still fairly novel. We had to discover for ourselves what her choices would be in all the different scenarios we could envision by talking to ambulance drivers, lawyers and doctors. A friend of mine who had worked in Emergency Medical Services for many years explained to me how limited their options are when they arrive after a 911 call. He explained that they wouldn't stop to consider written instructions, they are required to do everything they can do to resuscitate the patient. His advice for my mother and father was to only call 911 if they were sure they wanted intensive medical intervention.

My parents were practical in their approach, and not afraid to address the difficult questions. This is a letter that they had ready for each hospital stay or emergency room visit.

Barbara ♦ *February 19, 1991*

Power of Attorney

To whom it may concern;

My husband, Allan Feldt, has my durable power of attorney which names him as the person who will make decisions about medical care and treatment for me in the event I am unable to make those decisions for myself. In order to make it easier for him to express my wishes, I am describing some of them here. I understand that I cannot foresee all circumstances and contingencies which may arise. I trust him to work with my doctors and use his own best judgement in dealing with any and all medical care and treatment decisions which must be made.

Resuscitation in the event of cardiac arrest —
I would prefer that resuscitation efforts be limited to up to ten minutes of non-invasive procedures such as electrical stimulation, CPR, and injections of standard drugs. I want no invasive procedures such as cutting open veins and arteries for insertion of catheters or other purposes. I do not want my chest cut open for manual heart massage.

Treatment if in a coma or similar vegetative state —

Any procedures such as artificial feeding, water, or breathing devices which would prolong my life in a situation where I am incapable of doing these things on my own must be limited to situations in which there is clear and strong evidence that recovery is possible. If the coma or vegetative state appears to be irreversible, I want none of these procedures used.

Emergency treatment by paramedics and ambulance
personnel —

It is my understanding that when the assistance of an ambulance has been requested, emergency vehicle personnel are not permitted to follow instructions such as these I have written nor may they follow the instructions of a victim or her designee. I therefore have asked my husband to consider carefully whether or not to call for ambulance assistance. I trust his ability to decide when it is or is not appropriate to request such assistance.

One day you want to live, the next you want to have it over with. You go to bed brave, and wake up in the middle of the night terrified. As my mother became more physically disabled there was too much time to lay in bed and ponder it all. This was part of the reality for her. And for all of us around her.

Barbara ◆ *1991*

Options

LOSING POSSIBILITIES

1. Surgeon says nothing can be done. I am happy because I don't have to make a decision.

2. He can do surgery but I refuse. I feel guilty, cowardly, embarrassed.

3. I have surgery and it isn't successful. I become more of an invalid.

4. I die from surgery and it's all over.

5. I die from not having surgery and it's all over

WINNING POSSIBILITIES

1. Surgeon says nothing can be done. It doesn't matter because I do a lot of cardiac rehab and holistic stuff (visualization, etc.) and surgery becomes unnecessary.

2. Surgery is possible but I refuse it. I feel proud because I will take charge of my life — lose weight, exercise, do holistic stuff and get better without surgery.

3. I have surgery and it is successful. I get better.

4. I die from surgery or from no surgery and am reincarnated as a lovely, thin, healthy woman. I am raised in a family with a loving mother and a father who lives a long time. I marry a sensitive, loving man who doesn't drink. We have lovely children who don't do drugs and suicide.

A heart transplant may have been an earlier option, but my mother was ethically opposed to the use of scarce medical resources to possibly prolong the life of someone who had lived a good life, if not a long one. She knew that her refusing a transplant wouldn't automatically mean that there would be more money for prenatal care and prevention of disease, but that was where she thought the resources should go. With the later diagnosis of insulin dependent diabetes she was probably no longer a candidate. Whenever anyone learning of her condition proposed it as a possible solution, she used the opportunity to inform them of her opinions on the problems with the way that medical resources are allocated.

Barbara ◆ *May 25, 1991*

Regeneration

Quiescent on drifts of white sheets
life slowly dissipating
hollowed out, nothing left
but skin paper thin
as the shell of a pumpkin
abandoned in a snow covered field,
experiencing the satisfaction
of completion.

Breaking through fragile ribs
expelling fertile seeds
the careless step of a child,
like the surgeon's saw
preparing for heart transplantation,
initiates a new cycle of life,
new poems propelled like seeds
of Touch-me-nots to lodge expectantly
in fallow fields.

Barbara ♦ *January 19, 1993*

Expulsion

An amorphous dark gray blob
lodges between my shoulder blades
in a prairie dog colony
with burrows and passages
into my neck and shoulders
down my arms.

Amoeba-like it seeps
through tunnels
conveying pain
disseminating fear.

It explodes forward
into my chest
a deep purple flower
deadly nightshade,
valerian, spiderwort.

Asleep,
I pray it is hibernating.
Still it awakens
goes prowling,
stalking, preying
on my well being
threatening my peace of mind.

Then I gaze deeply;
perceive its dark shape,
vinegary smell,
taste of burnt toast.
It retreats
unable to survive
recognition, acknowledgment.

Dreams of Life

My mother was intrigued by her dreams, and the insight they brought to her life. She became adept at lucid dreaming, able to be consciously aware during her dreams and also to request that solutions to problems be revealed to her through this medium. There were many times she received guidance or became aware of deeper psychological traumas after a night spent dreaming. The two or three volumes of journals that she left were almost entirely devoted to writing about her dreams and what they meant to her. Almost no daytime events were included — it was all about what occurred during sleep.

This was the medium she primarily used to find completion in her life and to evaluate her progress in her personal growth work. The book that she started but never finished was organized around particular dreams and her interpretation of them, as metaphors for stages in her life and dying process. Much of the material in this chapter is from that unfinished book, called "Dreams of Life."

Barbara ◆ 1991

Introduction to "Dreams of Life"

People who have not learned the techniques of remembering their own dreams have expressed doubt about the validity of the dreams I have reported. They don't realize that we all have a rich dream life which can be captured during our waking moments. The dreams here are described just as I recorded them in my dream journal. I have not added or changed any details, although I have shortened some of them. I am not so imaginative as to have created these dreams while awake.

There are many theories and systems of dream interpretation described in various publications. I have presented the interpretations I arrived at alone or with the help of my therapist. Although I sometimes explain the basis for my interpretations, I haven't attached them to any particular theory or system. Other interpretations are possible, but preoccupation with the validity of my interpretations should not distract the reader for the discussions of the issues presented.

Barbara ◆ *1991*

Dreams of Life

Most people find it hard to think about death, particularly their own. Even though we are all dying, those of us who expect to die prematurely are forced to think and plan more concretely about issues that healthy people usually ignore. This is particularly true if you have heart disease because it never allows you to forget or ignore it. Angina attacks and irregular heart beats happen often and cause some degree of panic with each occurrence, no matter how many of them you have survived in the past. Someone has to decide if this is an 'ignore it and it will go away, a call the doctor, or a go directly to the emergency room' event.

In his book *Who Dies? An Investigation of Conscious Living and Conscious Dying* Stephen Levine discusses a Native American custom called the death chant. This is a healing device for "maintaining contact with the Great Spirit in time of threat or stress". One is assisted in achieving serenity at the time of death by practicing the death chant on each occasion when there is discomfort, illness, or pain. I thought it would be useful for me to have a personal death chant. I felt I understood its purpose but not the appropriate contents and considered who I might consult in preparing one. However, one came to me in my sleep and I had only to write it down on awaking.

When I get into trouble with chest pain or arhythmias, panic just makes things worse. So I have found it particularly helpful to use the chant to get calm in those situations. The first part of that poem is a visualization I devised which is helpful in situations such as lying for hours on a hard gurney in the ER waiting for test results to learn if I have had another heart attack. It is a wonderful way to go to a nicer place when unpleasant things are happening.

Its components come from several sources. The setting was created during my first experience with a mind altering drug, an injection of morphine to relieve the pain of pericarditis. I was hospitalized with a heart attack, very ill and very frightened. As I tried to relax so that the morphine could work, I found myself in a woods surrounded by birds and animals. They spread a carpet of grass for me to lie on and surrounded it with bushes and flowers. As I lay watching them scurry about I listened to singing birds and flowing water. Now I go to that tranquil place when-ever I wish to remove myself from situations such as the emer-gency room or the site of an unpleasant test or procedure.

My mother's death chant helped her through her near death experience and at countless other times. She practiced facing death with peace and optimism, and she had many (too many) dress rehearsals. Other cultures utilize this type of practice and perhaps the Tibetan Buddhists have explored and written about it more than any others. As it involves first acknowledging that you will need to use such a practice for real someday, I doubt that it will catch on in Western culture. The denial of the inevitability of death is woven into every aspect of our lives. Advertisers play on our fears, a fortune is invested medically to prolong lives that have been spent, and the sick and the elderly die segregated from the rest of the population and their "normal" lives that don't include death.

My mother was very excited about the concept of being prepared mentally for the moment of death. She called me to ask if I or one of my unusual friends could write a chant for her or had one already been written that she could use. I suggested that it was a personal thing, and she could probably write something for herself. She was interested, but skeptical.

That night she had a dream. Her "Death Chant" was written on a blackboard in the dream, for her to read. She woke up, wrote it down, and began to use it. I hope she had a chance to say a few lines before she died. I believe she probably did. The italicized part of the poem is the actual chant that came to her in the dream.

Barbara   ◆   *March 30, 1990*

Serenity

Pain awakened me at dawn
more piercing than shafts of newborn sunlight
challenging me to choose the right response.
Summon a screaming ambulance
for another jolt of scientific palliation?

Better to clasp the string of a shiny helium balloon
bumping its get-well message against the ceiling.
Float out of the open window
away to my secret nook among the trees.
Curl up in a mossy nest and eavesdrop
on morning murmurs of the birds.

Stroll to the edge of a quiet pool
gather up my burdens as flat stones
skip them away across the waiting water.
Stretch out on the sun-warmed sand.
Rehearse my litany to a listening spirit.

As I prepare to pass through the invisible veil
I open my arms to embrace new friends
I open my mind to receive new knowledge
I open my heart to experience new love.

I am content with the gifts I have received and those I gave.
I have touched many lives with compassion and love.
I have studied hard and learned many lessons.
I have used my knowledge and my love together
to make the world better than when I entered

I leave the world in the care of my loved ones.

Doubt and pain are born away
with the passage of Her healing breath.

Dreams were a way for Mom to try things out, regain control, and even to practice letting go and dying. They were also an avenue to accomplish things her body would no longer allow. Dreaming was a time when she could be strong, sexy, playful and adventurous.

Interpreting her dreams was a positive and empowering act for her. The meanings were usually clear, and often surprising and fun. If she was unable to understand certain parts her therapist would help her.

One day she felt great, the next she would have to spend in bed. Sometimes she could understand the logical cause and effect if she had been "overactive" the day before. Sometimes the way she felt just made no sense and no logical cause could be found. She rarely felt that she had much control or ability to predict how she might feel from day to day. This quixotic experience of health and disability was the foundation of her life for years, becoming more so towards the end of her life. Dreaming was a very vital and important part of her life. Her dreams made sense to her. Her heart was not as easy to explain.

Barbara ◆ *June 6, 1991*

River Dreams

The river is warm, brown
flowing slowly like maple syrup.
I am carried tenderly in its embrace
drifting through the featureless night.
I see the lights of a house glowing
growing as I approach.
I hear music, laughter, a voice
"Yes, she's much better now".
I see the dock, a landing place
offering food, drink, love
three strong strokes away.
I choose to float on past.

I swim peacefully in the warm river
toward an island of pine trees.
A clearing sparkles in the sunlight.
White coyotes romp in circles.
Attracted by their graceful leaps
I swim closer and see them pounce
on small animals, tossing, tearing.
The fierce heat of their breath,
their putrid odor, terrify me.
I churn away crying, "Help me.
I haven't strength to control them."

I am canoeing on the river with my lover.
It flows gently, we can choose our course.
On the near shore we see fringed gentians
luminous at the water's edge.
Above, black masked cedar waxwings
steal elderberries grown for jelly.
We cross over, propel the canoe
into the far bank where wild grapes
hang from tree strangling vines.
We pluck them into the canoe
plundering royal treasure
from the gold crested birds.

Control

Recurring dreams seem different from other dreams. Their message has a more powerful implication, just because of the many interpretations. A recurring dream —

> *I am driving down a steep street in Ithaca, New York in a VW bug. (In this case, down is very literal, since Ithaca is built on a series of hills surrounding the lake). I am helpless and terrified because I am driving from the back seat. I cannot control the accelerator, brakes or steering. Sometimes I am alone and sometimes my children are with me, but I am always in the back seat.*

Not surprisingly, I began having this dream when our oldest child reached adolescence. Almost overnight it seemed I had lost control of my orderly family life. Over the next few years the dream was repeated as another child became a teenager and things grew more out of control. Arguments and tears accompanied dinner almost every night. My husband had even more difficulty than I in coping with our altered life, and I became a buffer between him and the children. I tried to protect them from each other, to diffuse the anger, by keeping secrets. I listened to his complaints but did not pass them on to the children, and I did not tell him all of their problems and difficulties. It was a very uncomfortable position to be in, but I thought I was doing the right thing.

We had survived five years of courtship and seventeen years of marriage without serious disagreements. Now we were completely at odds over both the nature of the problem and appropriate solutions. While my husband believed the children had become basically bad people who needed strict discipline with appropriate punishments, I was convinced they had emotional problems and needed treatment and therapy. I could not admit that my children might deliberately do such terrible things. Although there was undoubtedly some truth in both our positions, we first became involved in various kinds of individual and family therapy. With little progress evident, both my husband and I yearned to escape. When he brought up the possibility of divorce, however, I had the last dream in the series. I was again driving the car from the back seat and this time it crashed.

Probably due more to their maturation than to any improvement in our parenting skills, the older children eventually became tolerable and even enjoyable people. They moved out on their own and it seemed that we and our marriage were going to survive after all. Then the youngest turned thirteen and it began all over again. But this time we were more prepared and we were on the same side - two of us against one child and no secrets between us. Family therapy was more helpful this time around, and our previous experience made us more hopeful of a good outcome.

Much to my surprise, I discovered that there was another, albeit extreme, way to regain control. When this last child was sixteen I had a heart attack, just as my father had when I was sixteen. This has always seemed to me a bizarre coincidence, although I obviously survived while he did not. He was taken to the hospital in the morning while I was at school and died in the afternoon before I knew he was ill.

The exploitation of serious illness to gain control is frequently depicted in movies and television, but I had not believed in it. Redd Foxx clutching his heart and saying "Here I come, Esther, this is the big one," to get his son to do what he wanted had never seemed realistic to me. I was wrong, however. People who had a glimpse of what it would mean to lose me treated me differently, even supposedly unaware adolescent people. Perhaps this is a result of everything but survival moving way down the scale in importance. Whatever the reason, my new dilemma became one of not abusing the enormous power I had so suddenly acquired. I had to resist the temptation to go roaring around in the front seat of a Jaguar.

Barbara ◆ *1991*

Packing Up

This series of related dreams has occurred over a two and a half year period thus far (it may not be completed yet). The first two are very similar.

> *I am at the home of one of my husband's relatives. We are preparing for a major family event which I am directing, organizing, and expediting. We are preparing large quantities of food and packing it into cars. I send people to bus, plane, and train stations to pick up family members arriving from all over the country. My husband is obstructing these preparations as much as he can.*

The next three are somewhat different from the first ones and from each other.

> *We are moving and the movers have taken most of our things. I have to pack the rest into the car. There is too much stuff to fit in the car. I am all alone, I keep finding more things to pack, including a large mirror, and I am very frustrated.*

> *It is Christmas and we are at Grandma's house. I am packing gifts into the car to return home. No one is helping and there is too much stuff to fit in the car.*

> *We are living somewhere away from home and it is time to return. I am packing suitcases and rushing to catch a plane. I feel very frantic and I'm afraid we'll miss the plane. I have separated things to be packed from those to be carried on the plane, but my husband keeps mixing them up. The kids are there, but not helping. There is too much stuff and I am cramming the suitcases really full.*

These dreams began a few months after my husband and I actually did pack up and move from our home of fifteen years. It is a beautiful old house upon which I had lavished thousands of hours of enjoyable labor–stripping paint from mahogany woodwork, painting, wallpapering, sewing drapes, and planting gardens. We were forced to move because I could no longer manage the stairs and I was very unhappy at having one more important part of my life taken away by my increasing debility.

Because of the gathering of distant relatives and my husband's unwillingness to participate, I assumed the family event in the early dreams was my funeral. The later dreams confirmed my interpretation that packing up was connected with death by acting out popular euphemisms and cliches. Trying to pack and move more than was possible seemed related to "you can't take it with you". Going home as a euphemism for going to heaven is prevalent in spirituals and folk songs.

While the general tenor of the dreams seemed clear, I couldn't understand the atmosphere of hurrying to get packed and get moving, the frantic rush to catch the plane. I didn't feel that in real life I was hurrying to die. At a weekend workshop on interpreting dreams I asked for help from the participants in understanding these dreams more fully. One suggestion was that I fear I will not die "well" in the manner prescribed by recently emerging gurus of death and dying, and I feel a need to do it now while I am still able to organize and control it. Another interpretation was that because I expect to die of the very unpleasant complications of congestive heart failure, I want to die now, before things get really awful.

At the workshop I also received some helpful ideas for making my life more enjoyable and less burdensome. A particularly sensitive suggestion was that I slowly begin to "unpack" my life and give my responsibilities and worries to others to deal with. I was encouraged to stop taking care of so many people and allow myself to be taken care of.

I have found this to be very difficult to do. For the first twenty-five years of my marriage I espoused a traditional woman's role. I rarely worked outside the home and concentrated on caring for and supporting my husband and children.

It is only in the past year that my physical limitations have forced me to give up both my work and many of my homemaking functions. I have found a strong need to find a justification, outside of my ill health, for asking my overburdened husband to help with shopping, cooking, laundry, and errands. I have found two that sometimes assuage my guilt. One is that for 35 years I have provided an uncluttered life for him by doing his shopping, cooking, laundry, mending, cleaning, bill paying, income taxes, taking his phone messages, scheduling his activities and entertaining his students and colleagues. The other is that when I asked him to resign from some of his civic and work commissions and committees to have more time for me, not only did he do so willingly, but he found tremendous relief in giving up the hectic life he thought he was enjoying.

About two years after the first packing up dream I had one with a very different tone and atmosphere.

> *We are moving and my husband and I are packing up our house. Most of the rooms are empty, but we go through them checking for items that may have been missed. There is no hurry and there are plenty of boxes to put things in. I find several blankets and fold them saying, "These are so old and worn I will only use them for moving and then throw them away".*

The novel features of this dream are the lack of pressure and the calm feeling. Also, my husband and I are working together. He is not interfering in my tasks and there is room for everything which must be packed. These are very different circumstances from the previous dreams, and my therapist pointed out the blankets might be transitional objects such as a child's security blanket. There is certainly a feeling of change in this dream. It summarizes the new level of serenity my husband and I have achieved in coping with the altered life style generated by my progressive illness.

I recently had yet another dream in this series.

I have only three days warning to pack for a move to another city. My small children are very upset. I am directing them to strip the beds and fold the bedding because the movers are coming. I find vases of flowers to be emptied and packed. Looking up at the top of the stairs I see a Christmas tree with decorations and lights which the children must remove. The movers are angry when they arrive and see how unprepared we are. I am very worried about moving back to Ithaca. I feel we have progressed too far to return to our old life-style.

While this dream has the frantic feeling of the earlier ones there is a significant difference. The pressures to hurry are coming from external sources, not from me. It is the movers who are angry and impatient. I think they represent the unknown and uncontrollable forces which will determine my time of death. Also, in this dream my children are actively participating in the final details of my life. I like the symbolism of the vases of flowers and the Christmas tree as the final things I pack up. I think they represent the beauties of nature and the family traditions which I cherish. My reluctance to move back to a former life-style may represent my current acceptance of death as inevitable but not threatening. I don't feel it is imminent, and don't wish to return to my former rush to get it over with.

After my mother's death I found my dreams to be an important part of learning to accept that she had really died. For about two months afterward I had a half dozen dreams in which I would be confused if she was alive or dead. I would see her body again, as it was the night she died, or ask someone if she was dead, or talk with her in my dreams. She would also die, then be alive again, and then be dead in a confusing back and forth that was hard to track. There has been no confusion since then.

Waiting and Wanting to Die

My parents wrote about what they would miss, and the losses they were experiencing. My father surprised us with out-of-character sweet love poems about the changing nature of their relationship and doing things without her. My mother's poems were more oriented towards exploring her ongoing depression, as well as keeping suicide as an option.

As time went on, their conversations shifted from "if I die" and "if you die" to "when." I think that close friends of our family may have gotten the idea that we were prepared for my mother's death. Things were in order, certainly. I had a plan for what I would need to do when it happened. I had a list of friends to call. I had thought about how I would handle my business. However, I was not truly prepared. I don't think it is possible. After thirteen years of "preparation" the actual death of my mother was stunned me, and was not like anything I expected or could have imagined.

There was a strong need to rehearse, to say the words, "well, once you're dead..." to Mom and to imagine. And yes, to look forward to when the waiting would be over. For thirteen years I knew that at any moment something unbelievably and irrevocably painful was going to happen. I was bracing myself all that time for what I thought would be one of the worst experiences of my life. I did not want Mom to die. But it was a reality so close — so near — that nearly every time the phone rang the thought came unbidden.

People we care about will die. It is a knowledge we all have, we all live with. I guess the difference was that I had so many reminders, usually every day.

Live and Let Live

Start with breakfast, everyone's
favorite; scrambled eggs or waffles
bacon, sausage, ham; butter drenching
raisin toast.

For dinner a perfect Manhattan
with a twist, rare prime ribs
a baked potato with sour cream
and butter.

An old friend arrives by evening train,
a glass of wine with a late snack
an intimate talk about the past few
months of her life.

Christmas Eve at daughter's new house
shrimp mousse, mushroom paté, herring,
Swedish meatballs, champagne, tearing
open presents.

At the Stratford Theatre's
twelfth row center for Brecht's
Mother Courage and Her Children.
sixth row on the aisle for *Hamlet.*

Old friends describe a trip to Rome
with a University alumni group. Eight days
in a posh hotel with daily tours
to nearby places of interest.

With a drawer full of
frequent flyer bonuses, my son
will fly first class to Seattle
to visit his grandmother.

The world is full of wonder;
things to see, touch, smell, taste
hear and love.

Sugar-free cardboard flakes
floating limply in skim milk.

Tomato juice,
broiled fish, plain rice.

Take six pills, then hurry
into bed like a six year old.

Same old hospital diet
Xmas celebration on video tape.

Wheelchair seating in the back
corner of Lydia Mendelssohn Theatre.

A "trip" of two nights at a nearby hotel
with mornings at a local museum.

A twenty minute phone call with
an aged mother after the rates change.

Let Dr. Kevorkian's critics tell me
about this life I should treasure.

Barbara ♦ *March 23, 1990*

To Counter Pain

Still with passing years I find
When in search of peace of mind
When all of life is too intense
Nothing seems to make much sense
I crawl into my bed and hide
Till comforted and calm inside.

When in psychic pain I vouch
For the comfort of a therapist's couch.
Sunlight patterns on the wall
Make a baby's crib so I won't fall
Into such a deep depression
I can't live till next week's session.

In the gazebo at the lake
I lie in a hammock for comfort's sake
Honeyed breezes wafting by
Bluebirds singing as they fly
Croaking frogs and whippoorwills
Cure my urban living ills.

Bed, couch, hammock, chaise, settee
All may serve to comfort me.
You'll find me prone to seek surcease
On any horizontal piece.

Barbara ◆ *Fall, 1990*

Indian Summer

We drove
along roadsides batik dyed
in variegated shades
of blue and violet asters.
Brown eyes
of yellow petaled sunflowers
watched frantic squirrels
gather hickory nuts.
Carefree canoeists
slid past cattail fuzzied marshes;
necklaces of sparkling beads
dripped from their paddles.

Delight
in the roadside stand's
harvest heaps of green
and purple cabbage,
sweet dumpling, butternut,
striped delicata squashes
is aborted
as bright bell peppers
green and red like Christmas ornaments
remind me of winter's coming,
too soon,
before I am ready to let go
of children in a field of jack-o-lanterns,
a black kitten purring in my arms.

Perspective

Old vows, lightly given in the flame of youth
take on new meaning among the embers of old age.
For better or worse. In sickness and in health.

For forty years we've shared problems, decisions, anger, love.
Children raised and launched, trips taken, adventures shared
victories won and lost, budgets and diets created and demolished.

As a lifetime together draws to a close,
inevitably, one of us must falter first.
New problems and decisions arise but shared in the same old way.

Prescriptions and dosages, doctors and endless tests,
hurried trips to emergency rooms, dull days in hospital beds,
watching yellow lines rise and fall on a more personal TV screen.

As old passions cool, a new union emerges.
Sharing yet again as husband and wife
the new and deeper meaning of the time that remains.

Allan ◆ *May 10, 1992*

Without You

After a motel dinner
I sit by the pool watching
the full moon rise slowly
through palm fronds.

Other diners pass by
talking with each other.
None look up to see
magic over their heads,

If you were here, would you
witness it too? Or would we chat
about nothing and leave
the splendor unnoticed?

Allan ◆ *February 3, 1993*

Memories

I want to remember:
> Dancing polkas, rheinlanders, and waltzes,
> Matching sidestrokes through chill lakes,
> Clinging to children as a toboggan swoops,
> Making love through long summer nights,

Still, I will never forget:
> Pushing a wheelchair along cluttered store aisles,
> Dialing 911 once again for yet another ambulance,
> Long hours spent in emergency room corridors,
> Holding hands while IVs drip and monitors dance.

There were losses of many types, and the need to tell other people as well as institutions of her change in status.

Barbara ◆ *September 1, 1992*

The Generic Letter

To whom it may concern;
Due to illness and increased disability, Barbara Feldt is no longer able to use the products available from your catalogue. Please remove her name from your mailing list.

Barbara ✦ **1991**

Suicide

I seem to be getting mixed messages about suicide from my dreams. In one dream, I am working in an establishment which serves meals family style to people seated at large tables. All the places are filled and there are many people waiting in line for service. I am rushing frantically to clear and reset places as each person finishes eating.

When I awoke from this dream I tried to analyze its meaning but couldn't. I went to sleep and found myself back in the same dream, the same room. This time there was a sign on the wall -

> *When you're done, leave*
> *so someone else*
> *can take your place*

I interpreted this dream as a clear directive to move on when you are getting in the way of others, meaning when you have become a burden to those who have to take care of you. Even though I did not participate in his care, I once felt a great deal of anger at a relative who lived for more than a year past his predicted demise from cancer. It seemed wrong to me that he would continue living when it was so much work for those who were caring for him. I did not want people to feel such anger toward me and believed it was my responsibility to kill myself before that could happen.

Barbara ♦ *April, 1990*

Therapy

Insulin shock therapy was formerly used
Like electroshock therapy to cure depression.
If you are planning to commit suicide with insulin
Be sure to take a big enough overdose
So you don't end up happy instead of dead.
Better yet, use a pen instead of a needle
Then when you change your mind
you have wasted only a piece of paper.
Gather paper, pencils, thesaurus and Kleenex.
Take them to bed with a do not disturb sign on the door.
Refuse to answer your doorbell, telephone, or husband.
Wallow in sadness, feel as depressed as you can.
Think about someone who killed herself.
Write a poem for her and one for yourself.
Even if your dreams are mostly about drowning,
Razor blades, packing up your life, going home.
Write a poem about a happy dream.
Recall something silly you read recently.
Turn it into a poem with a joke only you understand.
Get up, wash your hair, put on something cheerful.
Take a walk through the garden to see
What has bloomed in your absence.
Ask your son to bring a baby to hug.
Read the poems to your therapist.
Save these directions for next time.

In the previous poem, there are two lines referring to "someone who killed herself" and writing a poem for her. This is the poem. Sarah Power, a Regent of the University of Michigan, jumped to her death in March of 1987. She leaped from Burton tower on central campus. Her suicide had a profound effect on my mother. This was a woman she had met, admired, and perhaps identified with.

Barbara ◆ *April 9, 1990*

To the Unfinished Work for Regent Sarah Power

On my third annual pilgrimage
to place a pot of daffodils
at the base of the tower
I rage at the hundreds
who pass by without pausing
or remembering
when I still see the stain
and feel the impact.

Others occupy seats on the board
mechanically, lacking her passion
to right wrongs
to accelerate a society
which changes too slowly.

Where is the proposed memorial
a women's center?
The tantalizing prospect
of a safe place to gather
while storing up courage
to carry on her mission.

What future project
was written on her calendar
before the enigmatic message
conveyed by her leap
from that prominent symbol?
Does anyone truly know
what pushed Sarah over the edge?

This poem was written as an imaginary conversation with one of my mother's very favorite poets.

Barbara ♦ *February 25, 1991*

A Conversation With Maxine Kumin

"In *Feeding Time*, Maxine,
you described a daily circuit
through fresh snow to feed
horses, a dog, wild birds,
a cat, yourself.
And I sensed the completeness
of your life.

Memories of your children
were captured in blue bowls
you filled with soup from your garden
and with your love
of the earth and the creatures
which inhabit your portion of it.

I saw you so vividly in that scene
as though it were on film.
Is that what poems are?
Scenes from the movie of one's life?"

"Sometimes, Barbara.
But in *Indian Summer*
when you described the squashes
and bell peppers whose colors
reminded you of Christmas
and the coming winter,
it was not a movie, but a snapshot,
of a moment in a day
so painfully beautiful
you could not peacefully
let go of a purring kitten or of life."

"You eased your grief, Maxine
at your brother's early dying
by writing of shared childhood,
and of preserving plums from his garden,
putting some raveled things
unsaid between us into the boiling pot
of cloves, cinnamon, and sugar."

"Barbara, what have you written
to soften your despair
at the premature death
descending upon you?
The heart monitor blips,
the IV bag drips,
the nurses' shoes squeaking
toward your room?"

"You find my *Dreadful Poem* less elegant
than your *Retrospect in the Kitchen*, Maxine?
Perhaps that's not surprising,
since you wrote of another's death
after healing time had passed,
while I speak of my own death,
how it might be.

Wanting to be at home,
touching my loved ones,
hearing comforting words,
soft music in the background.
And fearing it will be
a failed resuscitation effort
among green garbed strangers
with only the words 'stand clear'
propelling me onward."

Barbara ◆ *1991*

Family Suicide

My husband and I have joined the currently active debate concerning the question of who has the right to decide that life is too unbearable to continue. After much discussion we have agreed that when that time arrives for either one of us, we will discuss it with our partner, but take sole responsibility for carrying out the decision to end our life. However, I insisted that we also make another agreement — that if one of us becomes totally incapacitated, but wishes to hang on and be taken care of, that will be okay, too.

There was a time when I thought that suicide was a more forbidden subject for discussion than the big taboos — sex and income. When our oldest child first attempted suicide almost 20 years ago, we didn't talk to anyone about it, especially to him. We thought that mentioning the possibility would encourage him to make other attempts. But as he continued to carry out acts of self destruction over the years, we were forced to discuss it with him and his various therapists.

We tried concealing this from his youngest sister who adored him, but were unsuccessful. She was already well acquainted with the subject and insists she first contemplated suicide a year before his first attempt, when she was eight. Although I am not aware of any suicide attempts on her part until she was in her early twenties, she certainly courted serious injury and death throughout her teen years by engaging in a variety of risky behaviors, including maintaining relationships with men who physically abused her.

I had several long conversations with both of these children as I tried to understand more about suicidal tendencies and to enroll them in my personal support system. They have each been helpful to me because their knowledge and experience far exceeds mine. I was unhappy to learn that their tendencies toward self destruction still recur and will probably continue to do so throughout their lives, but it is comforting to know that they continue to survive them. If I ever take up embroidery I will make us each a family motto proclaiming my favorite line from John Irving's <u>The Hotel New Hampshire</u> — "Keep passing the open windows."

Barbara   ♦   *August 12, 1992*

Essay

In the many discussions of the pros and cons of Dr. Kevorkian's assisted suicides, there has been little discussion of the fact that most of his clients have been women. I think this is an important circumstance which should not be ignored.

I believe that the upbringing and lifelong experience of women can give them a distorted view of their purpose and position in life. Women are the traditional caregivers; accustomed to caring for husbands, children, colleagues, friends and aging parents. When women become ill or disabled, they find themselves in a new role as care receivers.

This can be an unfamiliar and uncomfortable position and may create doubts about a woman's value to society and even her right to exist when she is no longer able to carry out that traditional role. Women then become vulnerable to subtle messages and pressures to end their lives, and may, more readily than men, consider suicide as the best solution to illness and disability.

If we are to legalize physician assisted suicide, safeguards must be provided to insure that women are not coerced into ending their lives prematurely. They must have easy access to the sort of care provided by hospice organizations so they will not feel their need for care is a burden on their families. And society must recognize the existence of pushes toward suicide which are so subtle that individual women may not even be aware of them.

We children were all aware that my parents had thoroughly discussed assisted suicide and had agreed it would be a lasting and loving act they could perform for one another if the need ever arose. If it had, they would have carefully orchestrated it so that no one could be implicated. They knew under what circumstances they would each choose to die rather than to live. They agreed to assist each other to end their lives if necessary. My mother was diagnosed with insulin dependent diabetes in the last years of her life. She felt some relief in being diabetic. Not only was this a disease she could finally control, but by stockpiling a bit of extra insulin in her refrigerator she believed that she could exercise her option to quit at any time.

Her natural death, prolonged and tumultuous as it was, remains my first choice in how to die. We would have lost so much of her and learned less if she had opted out earlier. Still, it was her right to have that option, and I defend her right to choose to die. I also believe that in her case, knowing that she could "pull her own plug" at any time helped her to survive longer.

Barbara ♦ **1990**

Untitled

Last Year

My aging body
    craved producing
      a child

Finding Peace

Sometime in late February of 1991, my mom called me. She was very frightened. Her kidneys had stopped working, and she decided to call me before venturing into the medical morass she was growing so tired of. I went over, and she was more scared than ill. She hadn't urinated all day and was bewildered about this brand new symptom. She was taking drugs by the handfuls, including diuretics, and we went over all the options about what might have happened.

So much of her life now was taking just enough medication to live, but not so much that it would kill her. Was this a side effect? A sign of her body saying enough? She had a hospital bed in her room, so that she could sleep partly elevated. My dad and I sat on the floor next to her, talking about life and death and what she wanted to do right now — and with the rest of her life. It was a teary evening, making phone calls to get more information about what was going on, and talking about her quality of life.

She called her cardiologist and within a half hour got the call back saying take more diuretics, drink juice, and wait. While we waited she eventually was able to express how she was feeling and the need to communicate it to her friends and extended family. Writing a letter began as my idea, and once she got over feeling awkward she could barely wait to begin its composition.

Later that night, her kidneys were working perfectly, and never again gave her any problems. This is the letter she sent out soon after.

Barbara • *March 3, 1991*

To My Dear Family and Friends,

This is a very strange sort of letter to write, definitely not one for which there is a proper form prescribed by Emily Post. But I need to communicate with you, my nearest and dearest. I ask you to forgive what may seem to be a stark and impersonal method. I don't have the energy to telephone each of you as I would wish, so I have chosen this way to express my thoughts.

My physical condition has taken a clear downward turn and I feel I may be running out of time to do and say many things I have planned. The doctors are baffled, because they can't find any measurable change in the batteries of tests they administer regularly. Since they can't measure it, I can't give you a medical reason for what is happening. I can only say that I know something has changed. I have more frequent and more severe episodes of profound weakness, days when I can barely lift a pencil, or even worse, a fork.

So this is what I would say to you if I could talk to you directly. I want to thank you for the contributions you have made to my life. Each of you has taught me something about living more consciously, more completely. You have taught me about loving and giving and sharing on a deep and meaningful level, and I thank you for those gifts.

I also have such wonderful memories of the time we have spent together, the fun we have had enjoying so many things - birds, wildflowers, sea shells, picnics, parties, card games, children, concerts, plays, restaurants, reading, writing, exploring new places. The list is endless and has made my life so full and satisfying.

As you know, one of the most consistent characteristics of this illness has been its variability, and we hope this is a temporary setback. But I believe expressions of love and appreciation are never wasted, so I am taking advantage of this opportunity to thank you for your love and support and hoping there will be many more.

There were many wonderful responses to the letter. It greatly raised her spirits and she experienced a surge of health. Here is one of her replies, to a distant long term friend.

Barbara ◆ *March 27, 1991*

Dear Molly,

Thank you so much for your lovely letter. I have good news this time; I am feeling better. Should I feel embarrassed at this turn of events? I don't, because I truly believe that all the good wishes I received are what made me better. The doctors sure don't know what's going on, but they don't know what you and I do about the power people have to heal themselves, and each other. It is wonderful to be getting out and around, driving some, not using a wheelchair much and not having to ask someone to do everything for me.

You are right in saying my illness has been a gift to me. I have felt that for a long time, and the main purpose I have had in writing about myself is to share what I have learned with other people. As a result of my letter, which a friend shared with a friend of hers, I am going to have more of an opportunity to do that. I got a letter from a woman in California wanting a copy of my poetry book and other things I have written and permission to use them and my letter in her work in bioethics. She wants to share them with people she is working with who are dying and maybe publish my stuff in newsletters, etc. I am very pleased. It is wonderful to know that there is a network of beautiful people around the country and the world, too, who share the ideals you express in your life of conscious simplicity and I have found in my efforts at conscious living and conscious dying.

Writing is still the major joy in my life, along with meeting wonderful people in my writing classes. I have found poems to be much like dreams in that they have a life of their own which reveals things I didn't know about myself. It is great therapy and

I have done a lot of work on dealing with my father's death when I was 16. Now I need to deal with my relationships with my mother and my children, and I am very resistant to that. Too much risk involved in digging into them, I guess.

I am intrigued with your question about why death is so sad. I have found that most of the time I don't feel sad, because what I will be missing are unknown future things which don't seem like very real losses. But once in while, like in the day I described in *Indian Summer*, something happens that is so perfect and beautiful I don't want to leave. Of course it is easy to see why the people left behind will be sad. I have enough ego to know I am important to a lot of people, especially Al. We have been together 42 years, and that's a long time. We have just come to realize that we were clever to get together when we were 16, because that has given us a longer life together than most people get, even if they live longer.

I am also interested in your idea about communicating from the beyond. I hadn't thought about that, but you remind me that it is possible. I certainly will try it, and I'll probably have lots of time to communicate with lots of people, so you will definitely be on my list. So far my therapist is the only other person to ask to be contacted. Meanwhile, I have been feeling better for three weeks and find that encouraging. I have no idea how long it will last, but I'm just enjoying it day by day. Thanks for sending the good energy which keeps me going. I think of you when I hear our little birds and love you for all the beauty you have brought into my life. I can't picture your children as they are now, but send my love to them and David. I will keep in touch. I think I would like to have your phone number, too. I would like to hear your voice once in a while. Some days I don't have the energy to talk to people, but when I do, it is always a lift.

I was somewhat apprehensive about the reactions I might get from my letter, but they have been mostly positive. I got one which describes part of my purpose in sending it better than I could. "Thank you for giving us all some warning that you might not get better so that we can begin to get used to the idea and so that we can be supportive." I am sure that part of the reason I am feeling better now is because of all the positive responses I got to the letter. I think it was a good thing to do, however unconventional.

Early on, she discovered that writing was also therapy. It was a vehicle for exploration. Sharing her words with others also helped with the isolation she felt. She had never been a very social woman, outside of friendships with my father's colleagues and later workmates of her own. She didn't have friends who were experiencing what she was. Having friends and strangers read about her life and feelings was also her way of opening up to others — of sharing who she was and what she was experiencing. It was a way for her to discover what she felt, as well as to express herself. She shared things in her writing she would never dare say out loud.

Sharing Writing

Writing was important to both Mom and I. From writing and sharing came the strength and perspective to live, and my way of acknowledging all that was best in her as she was dying those twelve long years was to support her and to share in her work.

I published three chap books of her poetry with help and illustrations from my ex-wife Shannon, participated in constant discussion and criticism sessions of her poetry, and attended creative writing classes with her at the community college. There I endured the kind words of those who thought it so "special" that I would push her wheelchair and help her to have this time to participate with others in writing. What they didn't under-stand was that it wasn't special for us, it was essential to survival. Divorce, disease, fear of death and loneliness, there was a lot of pain and reassessment going on that we shared those last few years.

From her I learned of other poets, styles, and ways of ex-pressing feelings that were too strong to fit into a letter or journal. She read other's works as fiercely as she created her own and assignments from her many writing classes inspired me as well when she described them. It's hard to express the sense of release I felt after writing the following poem about my feelings for Shannon after she left and I had to face the fact that I would now live without someone I loved so much and for so long. My mother's own thoughts about letting go and her joy on reading the poem and confiding in each other about how wonderful/ terrible a thing love was sustained me through both my divorce and her death.

David ◆ *Fall, 1992*

Pulse

This is a love poem
A gut shot, who's hot, do something stupid poem

Clenched heart, mind spin
I used to think I knew how it worked poem

Fight, die, rebirth time
pause for a commercial message rhyme

Woman seeing, hard blonde tears poem
Scuffed shoe, big change, fight back poem

I'm strong, you're wrong, so long feeling
I'm weak, you're sweet, lets meet reeling

Reach, drop, best shot, why not
True grit, don't quit, this is it
feel pain, big gain, sore brain poem

Love you, can do, not through
Try hard, pain scarred, back yard
rebirth, scorched earth, quiet mirth
maybe roam, miss home, love poem.

Barbara ◆ *1989*

Inspiration

On my patio
I settled in the most splintery chair
fighting to postpone restless dreams
of confinement in a narrow, barren space.
The cool landward breeze carried rustles
and croaks of nesting ducks and wooing frogs
as it flowed around and through me.

      I forced my clenched hands
      to open.

I am aware I must remain
where the music and the water and the wind
will find me, will flow through me, recreate me.
These are the wellsprings of my love
for family, strangers, friends
and for myself.
I need love most of all.

      I will use my hands
      to mold love into poems.

Out of the Valley of the Shadow

The wise and wonderful things I had rehearsed
    were all blown away.
No peaceful passing when I had forgotten
    my prayer.
Husband, children, parents, siblings, grandparents,
    grandchildren, friends.
I clicked through the register of people I loved, events
    of my life.
Serenity came from recognizing my contributions, telling them
    like a rosary.
Trees I saved with laundered napkins, damp greens dried
    on terry towels.
Frantic parents, troubled teens, hurt and angry clients
    I counseled, healed.
Reprieves for fledgling school programs bought
    with my reports.
Promotions for women and minorities compelled
    by my research.
Dreams and poems of my heart I shared to help others manage
    with their lives.

One of the most painful things for me in watching my mother die, was the feeling of being cheated. Throughout much of my childhood I had attempted to take care of her, watch out for her, anticipate and meet her needs. In my adulthood her illness again demanded thinking of her. I traveled less often than my friends. I cared for her physically and otherwise in my capacity as a health practitioner. As she became more disabled, I experienced her becoming more selfish and self-centered.

I saw my very last chance for having another kind of mother/daughter relationship, in which I was more often the focus of attention, fading away. My needs for attention, spontaneous affection, and loving consideration where going unmet by her. There was so much of my life that she didn't understand, and couldn't relate to. She had never lived alone, never established and managed a business, never had a life like mine. I felt that she couldn't listen long enough to know me. By the time I understood many of the dynamics of our relationship and how we collaborated in this role reversal to meet unstated needs, it was too late.

She only wanted to talk about her life, her writing, the praise she had received. She rarely asked questions about me and what I was doing — my hopes and dreams. She didn't even know something simple such as what a typical day was like for me. We went to therapy together, at my request, and this was one of the issues I presented in that setting. The therapist agreed that my mother could take more interest in my life. Although she agreed to the concept nothing changed. I still called her everyday and listened while she told me how brilliant and wonderful she was. Of course, I knew and agreed that she was talented and wonderful. I told her often, and enjoyed seeing her work whether she was being passionate or obsessive about it.

Each member of my family resented her preoccupation, while also grudgingly conceding the floor to her many times. We let her call the shots. Year after year. In retrospect, it was the right thing to do. It is likely that if she hadn't sacrificed so much of herself being a conventional wife, mother, and caretaker she wouldn't have had to claim so much of our attention and adoration at the end. It was only later in her life that she questioned how much of herself she had put aside because she hadn't known there was any other way to do it. This is a poem that helps explain her self-centeredness.

Barbara ♦ *April 9, 1990*

Should I Wear a Wreath

If you hang a mourning wreath on the door
of a house which has lost a person
where do you hang a wreath on a person
who has lost a house?

The wreath warns people not to intrude
on the grief of those inside
with requests to buy brushes
or contribute to the March of Dimes.

Should I wear a wreath to warn you
that when you admire my new ranch house
I may cry
because I still mourn the loss of my Tudor house
with mahogany bannistered stairs
I can no longer climb?

To warn you that I enjoy hearing
about your trip half way round the world
but I may weep
because I cannot travel across the country
to visit my mother?

To warn you that your pictures
of English gardens are lovely
but I may not see them
through my tears
since I cannot walk in the nearby woods
to see a garland of fairy mushrooms
encircling a decaying tree stump?

Priorities

Many concrete losses occurred in the years following my heart attack, including energy to do more than minimum tasks at home and work, the ability to travel, to enjoy favorite foods, and then to lose my house, my mobility and my job. But the greatest loss was the most indefinable — my future. For me the future was a hazy vision of things that would happen, things I would do. It was a feeling of unlimited time to work and to play, to relax and enjoy old and new pleasures. Time to experiment and anticipate new adventures.

With the heart attack time changed from a plentiful commodity to a rationed one, from something I never worried about to the thing I worried most about. Knowing my future was uncertain, it became imperative to make decisions about what to do with the limited time available. But how much time? Who could say?

My vision of the future included many years of working in affirmative action research at the University of Michigan. I had already seen policy changes directly related to my research findings. I was developing a monitoring and reporting system for discrimination complaints which would focus educational efforts in order to reduce such incidents.

I also imagined spending time enjoying my grown children. The hard work of raising them was over, they are productive and interesting people, and I was ready to reap my rewards. Of course grandchildren are a large part of the vision. I remember my own grandparents and the wonderful hours I spent with them. I want to bake cookies, have tea parties and sew doll clothes, take nature walks and do crafts with natural materials, play cards and board games, go swimming and boating. I would even like to have great grandchildren, as my mother does.

My husband and I had many plans to travel and enjoy recreational activities. His students issued invitations to visit The

Netherlands, Spain, Thailand, Taiwan, China, Japan, Korea and other exotic lands. We also wanted to visit friends and family all over the United States and spend time at other universities in Elderhostel or as visiting faculty.

We want to continue attending plays, concerts, lectures, and galleries, learn new hobbies like pasta making, expand our flower and vegetable gardens, and just spend years enjoying the fruits of our labor and our loins.

Now I had to set priorities. I had to choose where to expend my dwindling supplies of energy and hours. It was very hard to choose between my needs and those of my family, my friends and my work. I tried to keep everyone happy and it was impossible. I felt guilty when I put myself first, and unhappy when I didn't. I was selfish about many things, big and small. I wanted first choice in activities, control of TV programs, holiday plans, all because it could be my last while others would have years more to do what they wanted.

Sharing Yourself

Although I have met people who recovered and resumed a normal life after a heart attack, for me this has been a progressively debilitating disease. My doctor assures me that my level of health goes up and down, not just down, but I know that a year ago I was attending rehabilitation classes involving fairly strenuous exercise and now I can barely walk a block. I do my grocery shopping in a wheelchair and spend more days in bed recovering from a trip than on the trip itself. I can no longer work and find plenty of leisure to think about how I wish to spend my remaining time.

About a year ago my husband and I attended a weekend workshop on life and death where we learned a great deal from interactions with the facilitators and other participants. One of the first assignments was to give a list of the issues each of us wanted to work on to the facilitator. At the top of both my husband's and my list was "I need to talk to my spouse about her/my impending death but she/he doesn't want to talk about it." Needless to say, we talked about it that weekend and continue to do so frequently and openly. It is very important to us to share our feelings both verbally and through touch. We cry together and sometimes even joke about what we are experiencing. It has been an enormous relief for both of us to stop protecting each other from things we both felt but feared were too painful for the other to hear.

I recently reread *Crossing to Safety* by Wallace Stegner. I was profoundly affected by the ending in which a woman dying of cancer is organizing the circumstances of her death. She is maintaining rigid control of all the details of her treatments and setting rules about how people are to act around her and what emotions they may express. I found myself disliking her very much and vowed not to act as she had. It is impossible to legislate how people feel and a great disservice to refuse to allow them to express their feelings. The dying person is not the only one with legitimate and appropriate needs which deserve consideration. I am trying now to be sensitive to other people and not to let my need to be in control turn me into an unfeeling dictator.

Barbara • *February 4, 1990*

Entangled

Caught in the cobwebs of my room
are lingering remnants of a former self.
Power suits, tailored shirts, silken scarves
idle in the closet.
Dancing shoes, hiking boots, field glasses
gardening gloves, briefcase
rest unmoving on the shelf.

Held captive by that room, I am
accumulating accessories of a new self.
Television, healing books, meditation tapes
settle within reach.
Electric bed, oxygen tank, call bell
wheelchair, insulin syringes
redefine my life.

The rocking chair which once quieted crying babies
now soothes tearful friends who come to visit.

There were so many parts of life that both my Mother and Father had to come to peace with. Some were tragic, some you just got through, and some you could laugh about later.

Barbara ◆ *December 14, 1989*

Just Keep Laughing

It began when both awoke at 5:30 on their first morning on the west coast. He had been so eager to show her the sights the night before that he had pushed her wheelchair for miles on the crest overlooking the ocean. They had gaped like the tourists they were at the beach, the sunset, the walkers, joggers, lovers and even the homeless pushing their shopping carts toward nests among the trees.

Now when he tried to move, his calf muscles began to spasm toward painful cramps. As she gently rubbed his overworked old legs, he felt a pleasant and rare phenomenon arising beneath the sheets. How to use such a gift? She hadn't yet taken the medications which gave her heart a jump start each morning and probably couldn't participate vigorously in the obvious choice of activity.

Pain forced them to abandon a position which required using his leg muscles in favor of one which used hers. When she tired, determination and ingenuity produced other arrangements, all ultimately unsuccessful. After taking her pills, she rejoined him, literally, in a situation where both could rest but neither could move.

The closeness was still there, however, the loving touches and whispered words of affection But it had been such a comedy of errors that, despite her efforts to suppress it, laughter came bubbling up, breaking through in a giggle which became a full scale belly laugh. At least the laughter produced some movement and he enjoyed the stimulation of her muscle contractions. Accepting the situation, he told jokes to keep her laughing.

As the physical manifestation of his love ebbed away, their hilarity also diminished from a sea of laughter to a puddle of giggles and finally to occasional sighs of contentment.

Barbara ♦ *middle of the night — September 11, 1992*

Hailstorm

I twist ice trays viciously
snap cubes into a bucket
stomp down the cellar stairs
smash them hard as I can
against the stained cement wall

   crack crack crack

I pitch like Nolan Ryan
no one hits back
all out and still
no picking up pieces
it all drains away

My parents were not religious people. They had a profound sense of morality, social consciousness and humanity which they embedded in each of us as children, but it was not based in any particularly larger belief or dogma. My mother became more interested in spiritual consciousness as she explored what death would mean to her. Even then, it seemed that she wanted to know about the options, but never put her belief in any particular path or ideology. She knew she wouldn't have to wait very long to find out the truth, so there was no point in worrying about the details now.

Some of our most interesting and wonderful conversations were when Mom and I talked about her thoughts about life and death, and spiritual evolution. Much of our talk was speculative but I was also able to share ideas and experiences that were exciting to her and she shared her insights with me. On her own she read books and talked with other people in workshops and through her therapy. Religion had lost its meaning for her long ago, but deeper spiritual questions moved to the forefront as she came closer to death.

Barbara ♦ *April 26, 1990*

Meditation on the Master Plan

An extraordinary man
interrupts my view
of plump green juniper bushes arranged
against a background of grey brown earth.
A white beard frames his dramatic cheek bones.
Puffy cushions of white hair bounded by dark scalp
proceed down the back of his head
in a complicated French braid.

I call to him "Wait,"
I must grasp the impact of this design
which resembles the juniper bushes.
It appears again in puffs of billowy clouds
against a background of blue sky
and is repeated by cool puffs of breeze
interrupting the steady heat of sunshine.
Even silence reiterates the pattern
as it is broken by puffs of conversation.

Is there a message in the soft
impermanent wisps of shrubs,
hair, clouds, breeze, voices
pasted on the firm timeless background
of earth, scalp, sky, heat and silence?
Am I a part of that fleeting braid
on the back of God's head?

Barbara ♦ *September, 1992*

Dreaming of Paradise

I want to lie among soft pillows
like a pampered princess
pouring out profuse royal tears with
profligate abandon.
Ladies in waiting will lovingly
listen to my laments,
bring delicate linen hankies and
serve chocolate truffles
to soothe, console, and pacify me.

A prince in gold trimmed riding breeches
will carry me away
laughing in a charging chariot
to an enchanted land
no shots, pills, diets, deaths, divorces,
nothing to cry about.
I'll live happily ever after
singing, dancing, and composing
charming, lyrical verses.

But I will miss hulling strawberries.

The End

Linda Diane ◆ *November, 1995*

In the End — Shock

Shock. It can make people do strange things. It is the only possible explanation for what my father did. He let me know that my mother had died — by leaving a message on my answering machine.

We had even joked about it before hand. He had left me a message when his sister died, and I commented (sarcastically I thought) that he should not do that when Mom's time came. I never seriously thought it would happen.

I sometimes check messages when I come upstairs from a client. They have a chance to dress and regroup, I wash my hands, check who called, and disengage a bit from the intensity of working with him or her. Monday April 5, 1993, just after six, I finished a session with a new client . Things had gone O.K. but we hadn't made a strong connection. My father's message was on the answering machine. As I remember it he said, "Linda, it's your Dad. I think your mother is dead. She's laying here, her body is cyanotic. I think she's dead. Are you there? I'll call Ed (their family doctor and friend). Call me."

Everything slowed down. I said to myself "My mother is dead." I thought of my client downstairs. I realized that my mother needed to stay alive for another five or ten minutes, until my client had left. I resolved that, and went downstairs as though nothing had happened. Shock. It can make people do strange things.

I was calm as my client left. Her car pulled away. Now my mother was dead. I called my father. He was also calm. He said there was no need to come over, he had called the crematorium people who would be there soon. I became very resolved. I told him that under no circumstance were they to take the body until I arrived. He mentioned that he had called my sister, and convinced her not to come over. I told him I disagreed, and that I would pick her up on the way.

Her phone was busy, so I called a close friend and left a message (with his housemate — no answering machine) that my mother had died and I needed him. I left my dad's phone number.

When I reached my sister she was reluctant to come, as Dad had said don't. What good would it do? Yet, it was what she had thought was the right thing to do until our father convinced her otherwise. Did this come from his own grief or shock, or something else? We'll never know. We left for my parent's — now my father's — house, less than two miles away.

I don't remember much about the trip other than telling myself to drive carefully. A voice in my head was keeping me on the road, in my body, keeping us safe and functioning. Explaining to me what was happening.

My father hadn't moved her body. She was laying on her back in the living room on the floor, parallel to the couch. She was stretched out, wearing sweat pants and a sweatshirt. He had put a blanket over her. After connecting with my dad I went and looked at her carefully. My first thought was, "yes, she is dead." No doubt. She was gone. Not even slightly in her body. Her face was peaceful and only slightly — maybe distantly — surprised. I thought that her death didn't look sudden, but still not exactly what she expected.

There were the things to do, people to call, words we had to say before they came to take the body. I fell into that role easily — and was on the phone as soon as I could think of the first phone call to make. She had been scheduled to give a poetry reading that night — her first. There were details to handle. Should it be canceled? What about her friends who would be there? Somehow we arranged for one of her creative writing teachers to read her works. It would be awkward — "Barbara couldn't make it tonight because she is dead" but seemed the right thing to do.

I called my brother's ex-in-laws to find out where he was. We knew he was out of town, but we didn't know where. A short time later he called from Ohio and we talked briefly. He had a feeling earlier, similar to my own about the time she must have died. There was some comfort in the fact that at some level we seemed to have known. His was an urgent need to call her, mine was a feeling of unfamiliar dread and ill feeling that persisted.

Of all the things we did that night, my only regret is letting them take her body before my brother was able to see her one last time. I know that the experience was and will always be different for my father, sister and me, because we saw her dead body. At his request I described things to him on the phone, but it wasn't the same. And it didn't have nearly the same impact.

I went home, had friends over, ate chocolate cake, and had my friends call my clients to cancel appointments for the coming weeks. I spoke with my grandmother, and took care of other details.

Later, my friend put me to bed and with his help and encouragement I lost all semblance of control and rationality. I screamed and cried in his arms, hysterical with the pain of loss. It was an experience that took me more than a week to repeat again, sorely needed by that time. He slept in the next room, and sometime in the middle of the night I crawled into bed next to him for comfort.

There was still a missing piece. A few weeks later, I began to have strange dreams. My mother's peaceful death face became more haunting. I was confused in my dreams as to whether she was alive or dead. During the day, I could see the expression on her dead body and I felt uncomfortable with it. Something wasn't complete, and I began to feel that it was because I didn't know how she had died, or what her last minutes had been like. It didn't make sense to me.

In piecing things together, a few details didn't work. She had finished the poem and left the computer on, and David and I felt something, so we had an approximate time of death. She had started to use the toilet, but hadn't finished. She had clearly known something was happening — but went towards the living room, away from the phone. She wasn't crumpled like someone who had suddenly collapsed, she was stretched out on the floor. I needed to know what this all meant.

My friend Susun Weed came to town to give a workshop a few weeks later. We had time to talk, and I shared with her my discontent and asked for her help. Susun has a great deal of experience with death and a wonderful talent for blending intuitive knowing with logical information. She presented a scenario which seemed plausible.

She felt, from her experience and the information I gave her, that my mother would have known that this was it. As the intensity of the experience hits, one of the first things that a person feels is a need to defecate. There is a physical rush that affects the nervous system. She imagined my mother suddenly felt the urge and moved to the bathroom. Once there, she began the act but realized that her time was limited and that this wasn't the position that she would like to be found in. Confused and feeling pressed for time she got up and walked into the living room. Her plan would be to relax on the couch, to consider her final moments. Feeling a disorientation not unlike being very high on a drug, her depth perception may have been way off and she missed the couch. Not having the time or the energy to correct her mistake, she instead stretched out on the floor, and died.

I felt some relief in hearing this explanation, but not yet settled. That night I had a dream. In the dream, I was in the living room where my mother had died, and I started to tell my sister what Susun had told me. Midway through, my brother came in so I started the story over. Then, my father arrived so I began again. As I finished telling them all what had happened my mother appeared in the doorway. She looked at me and nodded, then was gone. When I woke up I felt at peace. I knew that I had the truth about what had happened. I never experienced any discomfort about how she died again. Relaying the story, with the dream, to my sister, then my brother, and last my father, they also felt the truth of it.

David ◆ *April 24, 1993*

Journal Entry

Monday, April 5th after a weird but reasonable set of meetings with CBIS and NYNEX in Cincinnati I went back to my hotel room and spent an hour talking on the phone to my friend Lori about death, wills and how to cope with feelings of loss, desolation, etc. Kind of prophetic as it turned out. Someone from the front desk came up and knocked on the door, telling me that my wife had called several times and needed to talk to me urgently. I called Shannon right away and she told me my mom had died and started to cry. I remember the next few days clearly, but it didn't feel like me saying the words or going through the motions.

All of the planes for Detroit had already gone that day, so I rented a car and drove back to Ann Arbor that night. The idea of staying alone in a hotel room in a strange city and going through the motions of business seemed pointless, although I was pretty sure I could do it if necessary. The drive north on I-75 was a nightmare and took hours longer than usual. I had to keep pulling over to the side of the road because I couldn't drive. Tears, the shakes, images of dad and my sisters sitting there next to the body waiting for the cremation folks to come pick up the body. Wondering how it felt to be all alone when you were dying, things like that kept blowing out my concentration and reflexes.

Since her death I spent a lot of time with my father and Linda and a little time with Laurie talking about things and working out details. My family is basically pretty weird, but I guess all families are at times like this. I was angry at Shannon for having poisoned our relationship to the point that I could neither ask for or receive comfort or help from her, but my friends stayed very close and helped in every way and at every time they could.

Over the next few weeks I got totally drunk a couple of times, spent very little time sleeping, spent a lot of time with my kids, got some good work done around the house, attended a conference in San Francisco, got some things straight with friends, had a weird talk with Shannon where she raged at me over things that made little sense and accused me of sending mixed messages about whether I was through with her, still cared for her, etc. Probably true. I guess her messages aren't mixed, but death throws a different set of light and shadows on everything.

I have loved and supported Shannon and the kids despite the challenges I have faced over the past 16 months, and moved far down the path of redefining myself and my purpose in life. Though thoughts of peace and calm come rarely and sleep is still awkward I am confident that I will prevail and be able to make a good and meaningful life for myself and what remains of my family.

We held a memorial service for my mother a few weeks after her death. She had the program ready, left instructions on where and on what day of the week to have it, and what music she would like to have. We each spoke at the service, the following is what we each said. I wrote what I had to say in advance, and gave a copy to a friend to finish reading in case I broke down. It turned to be unnecessary. The words that my father, brother, and sister spoke were less rehearsed, and have been transcribed from a video of the service.

Allan ◆ *April 18, 1993*

Memorial Service I

In case there is anyone out there who doesn't know me, I'm Allan Feldt. We do things a bit unconventionally in our family, including I and the kids are going to make some comments. We've been preparing for this event for some years. First and foremost, among the many things that Barbara had set in motion was a set of notes and instructions on what to do when she died. The instructions were to thank you all for coming and for all the support in the last years.

Administrative details first: there's a sign-in book out there, if you didn't sign it when you came in please do that. Shortly after this memorial service there'll be coffee and cookies out there, and you'll find maps for getting to the later recption. Also on the table out there, we ran off more copies of Barbara's last three books of poems. So if you don't have any poems and want them, please help yourself. And there is also a copy of the last poem she wrote, which she finished an hour before she died, according to the date stamp on the computer. Which was kind of a celebration of her life, it was about her 60th birthday. And it's better than any autobiographical statement I could make. Help yourself to a copy of that.

As you know, or you may not know, Barbara turned 60 five days before she died. We had a birthday party, a small party for a few friends and she died on the fifth. And in a sense it was the kind of death she would have wanted. She had been working on that poem over that weekend, just finished it up, it was lying on the table, I saw it when I came in the door, just finished, then I saw her lying on the floor.

One of the things she wanted to avoid was any kind of painful death filled with any kind of emergency situations. She died in a sense with her boots on, with her poem almost in her hand. That's the way she wanted to go.

You probably know that she had been preparing to die for some time. It was on March 10, 1980, that she had a near fatal heart attack. Since then every year on March 10 she and I would run off together and have a quiet dinner to celebrate one more year. And she's done well those thirteen years. This final step was not such a big one for her, she'd given up much of her life already. She wants us to celebrate her life. We're going to try and do that.

Three or four years ago, she wrote a short story describing Laurie's wedding in a kind of ironic joking way. Expressing her own relief and enjoyment. She enjoyed that story in particular and more importantly she found that many people were helped by it. Quite a few people said it helped them to better understand their own mother, and that inspired her to do a little more writing. She began taking creative writing courses at Washtenaw Community College, and found herself quite a good poet and has been improving over the years.

She has three small books of poetry and we'll put out a compilation sometime over the summer of some of her more recent works. And she has fans all over the country. We get letters from women we've never heard of because somebody has given them a Xerox copy of this that or the other poem. She'd been very surprised that word got out like that. She's also had a number of things published including an acceptance that came in two days after she died. So she was feeling quite productive, quite good, in the final years through poetry and was feeling quite good about the work she'd been doing on evaluating programs and so forth. She had a good life, and she doesn't regret, too much, leaving it. We're going to ask the kids to say a few words.

Oh I should point out, that on the program, the front page is a small piece of poetry that Barbara wrote some years ago, it's her death chant, a kind of meditation piece that she would read to herself anytime her heart was acting too badly or she was getting in a panic. It was one of her life sustaining things. The program itself was written by Barbara. We found a draft copy in her desk and a copy on the computer, all we had to do was fill in the date of her death. She contracted with Julie Austin several years ago to sing for this service.

Barbara, if you've ever worked with her, was very well prepared. The one thing she didn't prepare for, we had antici- pated fifty people at this service. There are seats for 150 and there are people standing in the back. I didn't expect this big a turnout. There are a few seats up here if you want to wander up. That's enough emceeing on my part.

Linda Diane ◆ *April 18, 1993*

Memorial Service II

Thank you for being here to celebrate my mother's life and to offer your support to our family.

In March of 1980, my mother had a heart attack that she survived. Thirteen years and a few weeks later she had another heart attack, which caused her death. What I mostly want to speak about today is those "extra" thirteen years of life, and how she used that time.

First and foremost, during that time period, she was able to have three grandchildren be born and become an important part of her life, and she of theirs. She certainly regretted that she wasn't able to be more active with them, but these three — Ian, Alex, and Graham — were a major part of what she lived for.

In thirteen years she also saw herself evolve from writing survey results and interpretations that were valuable to the causes of runaway and youth advocacy at Ozone House, to affirmative action at the University of Michigan, to a more personal expression of herself as poet . She explored her disability and threatened death, creating feeling pictures to more clearly understand her depression and struggle, as well as lighter pieces exploring the medium of words and cadence. Her poetry has begun to receive greater recognition, and is being used by many in hospice and counseling as a way into the grieving process.

In the last decade, my mother became absorbed with the therapeutic process, receiving therapy herself, and also involving all of our family at various times. In part because of this process, she experienced an evolvement of her spirit and greater peace and understanding of herself as a spiritual being, as a wife, as a mother, as a grandmother, and as a friend.

There were many things that she was able to accomplish in the last few years, ways in which she either facilitated or just observed greater balance and happiness in those around her. One brief example is that in a few of her many trips to the emergency room, she found women who were confused and scared, experiencing their husband's first heart attack. She would call them over, talk to them about her experience, reassure them, give them information and resource referrals, and her phone number if they wanted to call and talk later. She liked to help, to put things in order.

She also had the last thirteen years to be with my dad. Now this is the topic that she actually wanted me to talk about.

In many ways theirs was a traditional relationship. My father had the primary career, she was a full-time mother, the caretaking that was normal for a woman who had children in the 50's and early 60's. Even as she began to work outside the home beyond her volunteer activities, she still maintained her role as caretaker. As her disability progressed, this caretaking began to change and evolve. My father naturally moved more into that role, she began to let him into the kitchen, he started doing laundry and other tasks she had kept to herself exclusively. The superficial changes gave some hint to the fundamental ways that their relationship had evolved — and were a statement to their flexibility and devotion to each other.

It is a wonderful gift to a child — no matter what age — to watch his or her parents change. To experience first hand that the process of learning is never over. My mother, and my father as well, have added to themselves, added substance to their lives and to their relationship, in the last thirteen years. It has been a delight to witness that process. This is a relationship that has sustained 44 years of intimacy and love, and that is a fine thing to have been able to be a small part of.

In the last few hours that she lived, she was still able to accomplish things which drew her life to completion. She filed her taxes. She voted. My dad mentioned that, the night of her death, "she voted Democratic and then she died." Later, a friend who spoke with her at the polls corrected that statement by adding "at least we think she voted Democratic." When I repeated this exchange to my grandmother, Barb's mother, a consistent Republican, she sighed and said, "Oh Linda, we know she voted Democratic."

My mother knew she was going to die, and that it could happen anytime. She — and we — lived with this knowledge for many years. We had said good-bye many times, not knowing if it was our last chance to do so. Living with this knowledge was both agony and ecstasy. Agony in not knowing, in the impendingness, in the incredible roller coaster ride of emotions that she propelled us through in the last few years. The ecstasy was in the consciousness and awareness that facing and talking about death brought . The intensity it brought to our relationship, the intimacy that we had in this "now or never" atmosphere.

The morning she died, my mother and I joked about how one of the things she wanted was to "die perfectly." Of course. She was scared she'd blow it in some way, that it wouldn't be meaningful or right.

The only imperfection could be to not treasure the meaning of her life, and her inevitable death. And in her death, I experience that agony and ecstasy. And an inherent perfection.

The last hour I spent with my mother will of course be forever more poignant because it was the last time I was with her.

I was giving her a bodywork session, Monday morning, a few hours before she died. I ran out of time before I was able to give her a back massage, and she asked me to just rub some oil on her back as it was so dry. As I started applying the oil it occurred to me that I could just rub it on, be done with it, but I was suddenly very conscious of the act and reminded myself that even something this simple could be an act of love, could be done in a very conscious and meditative way. I didn't massage her, but applied the oil with clarity, letting the energy of love and deliberation flow from my hands. There was no impatience, and I was able to be fully present with her.

This was our final time together, and I'm grateful for that inspiration. It was a final reminder from my mother of the importance of consciousness, of truly being alive. And that is the primary gift her last thirteen years have brought to my life.

Laurie   •   April 18, 1993

Memorial Service III

Well, I didn't prepare a statement but I've been thinking a lot about what to say. The values that parents pass to their children from the time that they are born, those are what keeps that person moving along their path. What keeps them whole through all the traumatic experiences of life, public school, adolescence, all those things that our family in particular seem to have had some extensive problems with. We needed to have a very very solid foundation to keep us going. And my parents, both of them, gave me the most remarkable solid foundation of values, and all of the strengthening nurturing love I could ever ask for in order to complete myself in this lifetime.

The opportunities that my mother and I had for great tremendous intimacy are such a powerful lesson for us and when we meet again we will both be much stronger and better people for the experience of each other. And that is how it should be, and it happened, and I'm so very glad.

David ♦ *April 18, 1993*

Memorial Service IV

There are people way in the back there. All right! My father said we're kind of an unconventional family, so far this service has been a bit conventional. Might not last. We knew this was coming a long time. You probably heard that. But — damn! It doesn't change the shock. It doesn't change anything. There probably isn't a lot I need to tell. Most of you knew what Barbara was about. She sort of made you aware. Hit you up the side of the head with it or came forward very forcefully, and was not very shy about saying what she thought about almost anything. Including subjects that are a little bit touchy, like death.

And I think the thing that I was most impressed by, that I'm most touched by, the strength that I got, and maybe you guys can take away from this as well, is that when you're faced with something in life that you may not like, that may hurt, or may be kind of frightening and scary, like the fact that you're going to die, and when it's right here in front of you, maybe every day — for days or years or decades or whatever — she didn't flinch, she didn't say "I don't want to think about this" or "I bet someone will give me some drugs for that." She fought most of that way although she had well over 12 or 30 kinds of drugs they made her take because she was fighting to stay alive so she could fight to figure out what it was about.

Every minute, every day, the whole time she didn't give up. She spoke about it, she wrote about it, she talked about it. She did everything she could on every subject on everything that there was. People talk about sometimes blossoming, when people blossom in their life and stuff like that. I think Barb exploded. I think she got pissed when she found out that there really was an end that was coming and she might not be able to control or handle it. She got so much stronger and so much finer and touched so many more people. That's why this room is full and they're standing way in the back and probably in the streets...

You might want to think about that a little bit. When things happen in your life that are frightening or scary, they don't have to be death, they could be things much simpler or much more terrible. I don't know, it's not a continuum. I don't think there is a scale of living and dying. If we could all get that kind of urge, to not only make it work for ourselves but make it work for everyone around us as well, that'd be pretty neat. I learned that from her. Thanks Mom.

Laurie ◆ *February, 1996*

Journaling

February 14 — It was only two weeks ago, almost three years after my mother's death, I woke up and thought to myself, "my mom's dead".

I started to feel really sad. Then I thought "I don't have time for this, I have to get to my therapy appointment."

Hilarious, huh? No really, this is my life.

What have I learned from this experience? (My mother's dying process that is.) I have learned that the chances are good that children and parents don't actually know each other at all.

February 20 — When my mother died I became mostly disabled within two months. Almost three years later I am just beginning to understand the relationship between my mother's death and the fact that I can no longer rely on my back — my body's main support system. I have no idea of what the total relationship is between these two things. I only know that I'm very sure there is one.

I grieved when my mother actually died, but what has grieved me more, since then, is the shattering of my illusions or delusions about our relationship. I had believed that we had resolved most of our issues and that we had a really good and caring relationship. That we were important to each other. That she had finally realized that I was as important a figure in our family mythology as anyone else.

What I discovered is that everyone enters the death state alone. Whether it's a sudden or a prolonged process. External life fades and the inner process is the only subject that's lighted.

In life our perceptions are richly colored by self but we take much input from external sources. In the death process it reverts to all self.

February 21 — I can't help feeling that that person was actually a stranger. O.K. so I lived in her body. Maybe that made her feel like I could never be a stranger. I'll never know. I always felt alien. I have a hard time relating to the concept that we were ever that close. That she ever loved me and cuddled me and held me and gave unconditionally to me. It just seems hard to reconcile. Of course I turned out basically O.K. so I must have had this basic nurturing stuff or I'd have probably been hopeless.

She had difficulty expressing love. Even when she was doing an outward act there were barriers. Walls were up. She did what I do now, what my sister does to me. When a hug is happening the person checks out, maintains distance. Stays disconnected. She was so intellectual, so super involved externally, but not as there internally.

How could these people have just started in having children? She, totally hating her mother, abandonment issues with her father, resentment to her brother. Only the shining grandmother as any kind of positive role. Well, maybe that's why she wanted to be a shining grandma. I was just thinking "I'm pissed off at you. You crippled me." So how many levels is that true on? Why do these things just last and last. Not only last but go so deep into my body that I'm disabled.

Linda Diane • *November, 1995*

Giving away

> *More than anyone else,*
> *it is your siblings who remember*
> *how childish you once were.*

And my brother and sister have not let me forget it — nor I them. Now, with our mother gone, we had an opportunity to let each other grow up — and to demonstrate to each other our adult maturity that the rest of the world took for granted.

Our dad asked us to divide up Mom's possessions amongst ourselves. Within days of her death, my sister and I went through all her clothes, keeping a few things but mostly piling them in plastic bags to be given to a local charity thrift shop. We found one used facial tissue in virtually every pocket. As we tallied the value for my dad's income tax records for contributions we tallied the Kleenex as well. Searching the pockets — "O.K., and there is the Kleenex." It helped us to not cry as much.

Dealing with the jewelry and the family heirlooms my dad was ready to pass on was another matter. The stakes were higher, and all three of us would be involved. A combination that had never worked well in childhood and had rarely been attempted since adulthood.

My father was skeptical that we would do well, and my brother was adamant that either it went well or he would walk out. We spoke by phone the night before we planned to meet as a threesome. I tried to convince him that if we went in with the intention of it being a good experience it would be.

As we spoke, both of us became clearer about what our intentions and reservations were. And then, we formulated a way to make it happen. We decided, and my younger sister later agreed, that no one would be allowed to take anything. We would be givers. There was a wealth of interesting and important stuff — and we could celebrate the abundance by giving it away.

We would give to each other, to people close to my mother, however we decided. If something was especially meaningful or important to any of us we would speak up, but the decision on if that particular object would then be given would be made by the other two.

We had a wonderful morning. The attitude we shared was one of sharing, and we each felt acknowledged and treated well. Sure, each of us wanted the antique necklace from Israel. But I remembered how my brother had cherished it since first seeing it when my dad brought it home in 1969, and it was a pleasure to be able to give it to him after all this time. My sister received the "moon watch" that was my grandmother's, as partial consolation. I was surprised that both of my siblings were happy to give me the antique sewing cabinet I had admired since my mother had received it from an elderly family friend almost thirty years ago. Laurie was shocked and thrilled that she was given the antique cedar chest that she had wanted for as long as she could remember.

We went through the piles of things — enough for us, David's children, his ex-wife, Laurie's ex-husband who had remained close to my mother, and other family friends. When I got home, with all the wonderful mementos and practical items, I felt very good. There was no trace of guilt or fear of having manipulated anyone out of anything. I could have what I had come home with and enjoy it thoroughly. I felt given to. And I had loved the experience of giving to my brother and sister as well.

We had truly given each other the best of ourselves — and were willing to let each of us grow up and act as mature and capable adults.

Allan ♦ *May 1993*

Thirty-Nine

Over a month after your death
I've learned to live without you.
Cooking, cleaning, shopping, laundry
all fit into a weekly pattern.
Your papers are sorted and boxed,
jewelry distributed to children and friends,
wheelchair disposed of, oxygen tanks
and hospital bed advertised for sale.
Gradually the tokens of our
thirty-nine years together disappear.

But on the 39th day
I walk idly along a Florida beach.
Spotting a beautiful shell,
I pick it up without thinking,
in order to bring it home to you.

Afterward

I am no longer afraid of death. I am sometimes afraid of dying, but feel that this is an appropriate response to the vulnerability that is inherent in being human. The fear of dying is likely an innate biological thing. I suspect that the fear of death that so pervades our culture comes from elsewhere. Fear and confusion in coping with death is the linking element in our present paralysis in coping with the questions of euthanasia, abortion, what care to give to terribly premature babies, and even our unconsciousness of the treatment and means of death of the animals that are eaten. The prevalence of death, in war, disease, violence in the inner cities, or the death of someone close to us, are topics that seem to frighten most people.

I was able to observe the change my mother went through after her near death experience. She was no longer afraid of being dead — though she remained afraid of the circumstances under which she would die. The ability to accept death as a necessary and important part of life enhances that life. Our family's identity for thirteen years revolved around the precious and unknown quantity of life that remained for my mother. Often more than we wished it to, but that identity was hard to be free of for any length of time. Indeed, it was an important underlying factor in why we all ended up staying in the same city, all on the same west side of our hometown.

Being part of a conscious death is a life changing experience for the survivors. My mother gave me — and the rest of our family — that gift. I am so glad it is over. The waiting, the late night calls, the living on the edge, the pressure of knowing that every conversation might be the last — the one to remember for the rest of my life. It was a draining and life altering experience. After nearly three years since her death I am just beginning to be able to let the phone ring in the middle of the night. I am leaving home for pleasure and work, knowing that I am unlikely to be summoned back by some emergency. What a relief.

I miss my mother. It is a pain that I have found that few people really understand, mostly only those who have also experienced this loss. It's a bit like joining a very small and exclusive club. The membership dues are rather staggering, and we will all eventually be members. Unless, like my mother, you die before your mother.

Even after three years, there are some events that reduce me to sobbing. My mother will never meet the man that I hope I will eventually meet and become partners with. If I have children, as I hope to, they will not know their grandmother. She so enjoyed that role. These two thoughts are perhaps the most painful.

Yet, while one part of me wishes that my mom was still here, another recognizes that her time was over. She was so focused on the dying process. I may wonder how she would react to current events, what insight or experience she might share with me, but she is irrevocably gone. She was ready to leave, even if I'm still getting used to her not being here.

The publication of this book would have been a dream come true for my mother. She'll never know. But it feels as though at some level, as I live through the legacy that she left and express her dreams in this limited way, she does know. It is a continuation of her spirit. She is in this book. She knows.

I don't want to die. Not yet. The thought that my life may be taken early, by accident, strange disease, or violence, does bother me. It should, as I am young and have a great deal more on my agenda. Even to die as young as my mother was, just past sixty, bothers me a lot. I exercise, eat well, laugh often, handle stress, glad that these things enhance my life as well as probably prolonging it.

There is a lot we can do so that each of us die as well as possible. We have much more control and choice in the matter than it would seem. And death will come. It may be long and drawn out, as my mother's was, it may be quick and unexpected. Death is such a tremendous transition that explaining it has confounded philosophers, scholars and scientists. Exploring the concept of death and what it means has spawned dozens of fervently held religious beliefs. It is not something to be entered into haphazardly, with denial, or without preparation.

Coping with the death of friends, family, role models, and others becomes a more frequent event as we age. It is an integral part of life.

My mother is dead. Death is my intimate ally.

I am no longer afraid.